For the Love of Life

ERICH FROMM

Translated from the German by
Robert and Rita Kimber

Edited by
Hans Jürgen Schultz

THE FREE PRESS
A Division of Macmillan, Inc.
NEW YORK

The Free Press
A Division of Macmillan, Inc.
866 Third Avenue, New York, N.Y. 10022

Collier Macmillan Canada, Inc.

Printed in the United States of America

printing number
1   2   3   4   5   6   7   8   9   10

Library of Congress Cataloging-in-Publication Data

Fromm, Erich
    For the love of life.

    Translation of: Uber die Liebe zum Leben.
    Includes index.
    1. Psychoanalysis—Addresses, essays, lectures.
2. Humanism—Addresses, essays, lectures. 3. Per-
sonality—Social aspects—Addresses, essays, lectures.
4. Life—Addresses, essays, lectures. 5. Civilization,
Modern—20th century—Addresses, essays, lectures.
I. Schultz, Hans Jürgen.   II. Title.
BF175.F79313   1986   150.19′57   85-20518
ISBN 0-02-910930-2

Contents

Foreword

THESE REFLECTIONS BY ERICH FROMM are from the eighth, and last, decade of his life. His work was never done. He kept reading, writing, planning, learning; he remained open and curious to the very end. But the life's work that he left behind in ten volumes reached its high point and its conclusion in his last decade, and he drew on that body of work whenever he spoke as an alert and critical commentator on our times. What the radio meditations preserved here offer us then is an interesting supplement to his work. Their value does not lie so much in their novelty as in their vitality, in their characteristic expression of his deeply held convictions. Most of these talks were recorded in Fromm's apartment in Locarno, the remainder in our studio in Zürich. In reading them we can experience vicariously those meetings and conversations to which the great old man so graciously invited us.

Apart from some early works, written in a dense, academic German, Fromm's writings are known to us here in Germany only as translations from the English. In these radio talks, however, he comes back to his mother tongue; and his style—free of the restrictions imposed by paper—has a remarkable immediacy to it. Matthias Claudius once remarked that the written language is a diabolic funnel that converts wine to water. Fromm, too, preferred the spoken word, direct address. Here we have his spoken word. And anyone who ever experienced his speech will hear it again in reading these talks.

My first meeting with him was in 1970. We met, as we would often again later, in the Storehen in Zürich. He had his favorite hotels everywhere, and it is impossible to imagine his ever willingly relinquishing the role of host. We talked about the series of talks on affluence and ennui that he would record for us the next day at our Zürich studio. He sat across from me with his customary intent look on his face. Completely undisturbed by the hustle and bustle around him, he outlined his ideas for the talks for me. When he was done, I thought: Well, that's that. But no. Now it was my turn. He asked for my objections and, more important still, for information on what kind of audience he would presumably be addressing. With persistence and with questions that revealed just how familiar he was with life in Germany he meant to draw as close as he could to his listeners. To speak their language, but not to tell them just what they want to hear—that was his motto. He was very well prepared. He had an intimidatingly large pile of notes and drafts with him, and he added to them constantly as we talked. But the next morning he appeared without any of that baggage. I asked whether he didn't want to take his briefcase along. Amused, he shook his head. We drove to the studio. Without further ado he sat down in front of the microphone and, speaking extemporaneously, delivered his six installments, each one lasting exactly twenty-nine minutes. The only condition he had made was that I be present. He needed someone to address, a representative of his anonymous audience. Hearing formulations that are both spontaneous and concentrated is a joy that we in radio rarely experience.

While Erich Fromm was dealing with his subject and taking me along on his extensive Socratic journey, I began to notice that something was happening behind the glass that separated us from the control room. Even though Fromm was relatively unknown in Europe at the time, word had gotten around in the Zürich studio that something worth listening to was going on here. Technicians, secretaries, the janitor, and even some of my colleagues from the editorial offices gathered in the control room, stood jammed in together, and listened attentively. I personally feel that radio's potential for "dialogue" with the audience is very limited indeed.

We mustn't expect too much of radio or push it beyond the limits of that potential. We try to find a style of indirect speech suitable to the medium. But Fromm proved to be the exception to my rule. He displayed a refreshing indifference toward the instruments of the trade, remained unintimidated by them, and simply hopped over all the obstacles the medium put in his way. How did he manage that? Dialogue was an integral part of Fromm's thinking. His invisible listener was not present to him merely as a mental stage prop. His listener and what his listener might have to say in response to him were built-in realities in his thought. He could listen as he talked. He was a remarkably good speaker because he was such a remarkably good listener.

In Fromm the writer and the man were, to a remarkable degree, one and the same person. The one interpreted the other. His voice was the incarnation of his language. Fromm grew up in a culture with a strong oral component, the Jewish tradition. His entire work plays variations on a theme. It is full of repetitions, of new runs at old problems, new attempts to probe deeper, to elucidate with greater clarity. Very few scholarly writers are as given to a fine excess as he. For him, a lack of superabundance would be an admission of poverty. When I read him, I am struck again and again by the profusion of idea, suggestion, insight, interpretation. The reader is presented with an unending flow of example and evidence, and the scales fall from his eyes.

He loved to tell stories, either in response to questions or as a means of solving intellectual problems, stories like the one about a man who traveled a long way to visit a Hasidic master. When asked if he had taken the trouble to study the master's doctrines, the man replied, "Oh, no, I just wanted to see how he ties his shoes." This little story reminds us that a gesture will often tell us more than a lecture can. It also reminds us that the most brilliant remarks are of no use if the man who utters them is not the right kind of man. Whenever I visited Erich Fromm, I was reminded of that story. I always felt that I went away from him a different man from the one I had been when I arrived: I went away with my head clearer, feeling more alive and less intimidated by the forces that oppress us and make us vulnerable to despair.

It was not just learning that made him such an appealing figure. It was the interplay of life with theory, of theory with life. To be alive means to be reborn over and over again. It is a tragedy, Fromm writes, that most of us die before we have begun to live.

Insights like that are not the kind on which systems are built. What they demand of us instead is that we constantly see things afresh, constantly develop new approaches. Fromm did not want disciples; he did not want to found a school. A spirit like his expends itself fully to avoid being co-opted. He observed of himself, with no small pleasure, that his capacity for abstract thought was minimal. The only way he could think philosophically was in concrete terms.

In the late evening on January 5, 1974, South German Radio broadcast the autobiographical sketch "In the Name of Life." In the course of two leisurely hours, Erich Fromm told us things about himself that would never have been recorded were it not for this program. An actress who was playing in the Stuttgart production of Lessing's classic drama *Nathan der Weise* (*Nathan the Wise*) at the time came home from the theater, turned on her radio, heard the program, and then called me right away, despite the hour, to share her feelings with me. She had left one Nathan, she said, only to find herself in the presence of another.

Fromm was neither sorcerer nor scholastic. His talent for letting the heart speak along with the mind is a quality that used to go under the name of wisdom.

HANS JÜRGEN SCHULTZ

Affluence and Ennui
in Our Society

The Passive Personality

If we are going to talk about "affluence and ennui," then it seems useful to me to make some preliminary remarks about the meanings of those words. Clarity about definitions is crucial in any discussion, this one included. If we grasp the meaning of a word in all its ramifications and connotations, then we can often better understand certain problems that are circumscribed by that word. Its definition and history help our understanding.

The phrase "the affluent society" has stuck with us ever since John Kenneth Gailbraith's book of that title appeared in 1958. "Affluence" derives from the same Latin verb (*fluere,* to flow) that "fluid" does, and it means, quite literally, an overflow. But, as we are all aware, an overflow can be either good or bad. If the Mississippi River overflows its banks in a flood, that is a disaster. But if a farmer has a bumper crop and his grain bins are full to overflowing, that is good. "Affluence," then, is an ambiguous term. It can suggest the abundance that makes life a pleasure rather than a struggle for mere survival, or it can mean superfluity, an overwhelming and even fatal excess.

1

There is nothing ambiguous about "abundance" and "superfluity," even though there is little difference in their root meanings. "Abundance" comes to us from the Latin word *unda* (wave), which English still retains in its basic meaning in words like "undulate" and "undulant." Abundance, too, means an "overflowing," yet it has acquired an altogether positive meaning in our language. An abundant land provides us with more than just the basic necessities. It is a land of plenty, what the Old Testament describes as "a land flowing with milk and honey." Or suppose you have been to a party where there was no scarcity of refreshments. You might say, "The wine flowed in abundance," and you would mean something positive by that. There was no shortage of good things, no rationing, no need to worry about overdoing today and going without tomorrow.

But if we want to suggest the negative aspects of an "overflowing," the word that comes to mind is "superfluous." That word, like "affluent," goes back to the Latin verb *fluere,* and a superfluity is therefore a "super-flowing." Here, however, the overflow is seen in a strictly negative light. It is pointless, wasteful. If you say to someone, "Your presence here is superfluous," you're really saying, "Why don't you go away?" You are not saying, "How nice that you're here," which is what you do mean, more or less, if you speak of wine being present in abundance. So whenever we speak of affluence, we have to ask ourselves whether we mean a positive, enlivening abundance or a negative, deadening superfluity.

Turning now to "ennui," we find that its basic meaning is stronger than our current definition of boredom or a feeling of dissatisfaction and weariness. Ennui and the English word "annoy" both derive from the Latin *inodiare,* "to make loathsome or hateful."

We might ask ourselves now, taking our clues from these words we have just examined, whether superfluity doesn't lead to boredom, disgust, and hatred. If so, then we should ask ourselves some hard questions about our affluent society. By "we" I mean modern industrial society as it has developed in the United States, Canada, and Western Europe. Do we live in affluence? Who in our society lives in affluence, and what kind of affluence is it, an affluence of abundance or an affluence of superfluity? To put the question more simply yet: Is it good affluence or bad affluence? Does our affluence produce ennui? Does affluence necessarily produce ennui? And what would a good, abundant, ebullient kind of affluence look like, an affluence that does not produce ennui? Those are the questions I mean to discuss here.

But first let me make a preliminary remark bearing on psychology. Because I am a psychoanalyst, I will be touching on psychological questions again and again in the course of these remarks, and I want you to understand from the outset that my point of view is that of depth psychology or, to use another term for the same thing, of psychoanalysis. I'd like to mention briefly a point that will be familiar to many of you: There are two possibilities, two approaches to the psychological study of the human psyche. At the moment academic psychology studies human beings primarily from the standpoint of behaviorism. In other words, such study is limited exclusively to what can be directly seen and observed, to what is visible and what can therefore be measured and weighed, for whatever cannot be directly seen and observed cannot be measured or weighed either, at least not with sufficient precision.

Depth psychology, the psychoanalytical method, proceeds differently. It has different goals. It does not limit its study of human actions and behavior solely to what can be seen. It inquires instead into the nature of behavior, into the motives underlying behavior. Let me give a few examples of what I mean. You can describe, for instance, a person's smile. That is an action that can be photographed, that can be described in terms of the musculature of the face, and so on. But you know very well that there are differences among the smile of a salesgirl in a shop, the smile of someone who is antagonistic toward you but wants to hide his antagonism, and the smile of a friend who is happy to see you. You are able to distinguish among hundreds of kinds of smiles that take rise from different psychic states. They are all smiles, but the things they express can be worlds apart. No machine can measure or even perceive those differences. Only a human being who is not a machine—you, for example—can do that. You observe not only with your mind but also, if I may be allowed such an old-fashioned expression, with your heart. Your whole being comprehends what transpires before it. You can sense what kind of smile you're seeing. And if you can't sense things like that, then you'll be in for a lot of disappointments in your life.

Or take a very different kind of behavior: the way someone eats. All right, so someone eats. But *how* does he eat? One person wolfs his food down. Another person's manner at table reveals that he is pedantic and attaches great importance to doing things in an orderly fashion and cleaning up his plate. Still another eats without haste, without greediness. He enjoys his food. He simply eats and takes pleasure in eating.

Or take still another example. Someone bellows and turns red in the face. You conclude he is angry. Surely he is angry. But then you take a little closer look at him and ask yourself what it is this person is feeling (perhaps you know him fairly well), and suddenly you realize that he is afraid. He is frightened, and his rage is simply a reaction to his own fear. And then you may look even deeper still and realize that this is a human being who feels thoroughly helpless and powerless, someone who is afraid of everything, of life itself. So you have made three observations: that he is angry, that he is afraid, and that he feels a profound sense of helplessness. All three observations are correct. But they relate to different levels of his psychic structure. The observation that takes in his sense of powerlessness is the one that registers most profoundly what is going on inside him. The observation that takes in nothing but his rage is the most superficial. In other words, if you react by flying into a rage as well and see nothing but an angry person in the other individual, then you have failed to see him at all. But if you can look behind the façade of the angry person and see the frightened one, the one who feels helpless, then you will approach him differently, and it may happen that his anger will subside because he no longer feels threatened. From a psychoanalytical point of view, what interests us in everything we shall discuss here is not primarily (and certainly not exclusively) human *behavior* viewed from the outside but rather what *motives* a person has, what his intentions are, whether he is conscious of them or not. We are interested in the quality of his behavior. A colleague of mine, Theodor Reik, once said: "The analyst listens with a third ear." He was absolutely right. Or we might also say, to use a more familiar expression, that he reads between the lines. He sees not only what is offered him directly but perceives something more in what is offered and observable. He sees into the heart of the personality whose every action is merely an expression, a manifestation, yet one that is always colored by the entire personality. Every last bit of behavior is a gesture originating in one specific human individual and in no other, and that is why there are no two human actions that are identical, any more than there are two identical human beings. They may resemble each other;

4

they may be related; but they are never the same. There are no two people who raise a hand in exactly the same way, who walk the same way, who tilt their heads in the same way. That is why you can sometimes recognize a person by his gait even though you have not yet seen his face. A gait can be as characteristic for a person as his face, sometimes even more so, for it is more difficult to alter a gait than the expression of the face. We can lie with our faces. That is a capability we have that animals do not. It is more difficult to lie with one's body, though that too can be learned.

After these introductory remarks, I would like to turn now to the question of *consumerism* as a psychological—or, more correctly—a psychopathological problem. You may ask, What's the point of that? We all have to be consumers. Everyone has to eat and drink. We need clothes, a place to live. In short, we need and make use of a great many things, and that phenomenon we call "consuming." Where is the psychological problem in that? That's just the way of nature: We have to consume to live. Granted, but in saying even that much we have already arrived at the point I want to make: There is consuming and consuming. There is a kind of consuming that is compulsive and that arises from greed, a compulsion to eat, buy, own, use more and more.

Now you may ask: Isn't that normal? After all, don't all of us want to add to what we have? The problem, if there is one, is that we don't have enough money, not that there's anything wrong with the desire to own more and more. . . . I realize very well that many of you feel this way. But perhaps an example will show that the issue is not as simple as it may look at first glance. My example is one that will be familiar to you, but I hope very few of you are personally affected by it. Consider someone who is suffering from obesity, someone who simply weighs too much. Obesity can be caused by a glandular malfunction, but more often than not it is simply the result of overeating. The obese person has a snack here, a snack there; he has a weakness for sweets; he is always nibbling on something. And if you look more closely, you'll see not only that he is constantly eating but that he is driven to eat. He *has* to eat. He can't stop eating any more than some smokers can stop smoking. And you know that people who do stop smoking will often start to eat more. They excuse themselves by saying that anyone who quits smoking automatically gains weight. And that is one of the common rationalizations people give for not giving up smoking. Why do we cling to those rationalizations? Because the same need to take something into our mouths, to consume things, finds expression in eating, in smoking, in drinking, or in buying things.

Doctors are constantly warning people who eat, drink, and smoke compulsively that they may die prematurely of a heart attack. If those people act on their doctors' warnings and stop their habits, they often suddenly succumb to attacks of anxiety, insecurity, nervousness, depression. Here we see a remarkable phenomenon: Not eating, not drinking, not smoking can make people afraid. There are people who eat or buy things not to eat or to buy but to quell their feelings of anxiety or depression. Increased consumption offers them a way out of their dejection. Consuming promises healing, and in fact satisfying that kind of hunger does bring some relief from underlying depression or anxiety. Most of us know from our own experience that if we are feeling nervous or depressed we are more prone to go to the refrigerator and find what feels like relief in eating or drinking something for which we have no real appetite. In other words, eating and drinking can actually take over the function of a drug, acting like a tranquilizer. And food and drink are more pleasant because they taste good as well.

A depressed person feels something like a vacuum inside him, feels as if he were paralyzed, as if he lacked what it takes to act, as if he could not move properly for lack of something that might set him in motion. If he consumes something, the sense of emptiness, paralysis, and weakness may leave him temporarily, and he may feel: I am someone after all; I have something in me; I'm not a nothing. He fills himself with things to drive out his inner emptiness. He is a *passive* personality who senses that he amounts to very little and who represses those inklings by consuming, by becoming *Homo consumens*.

I have just introduced the concept of the "passive personality," and you will want to know what I mean by that. What is passivity? What is activity? Let me begin with the modern definitions of passivity and activity, definitions that will be quite familiar to all of you. Activity is understood to mean any goal-oriented action that requires energy. It can be either physical or mental work, and it can include sports as well, for we generally think of sports in a utilitarian way, too: Participation in them either promotes health or enhances the prestige of our country or makes us famous or earns us money. It is usually not pleasure in the game itself that moves us to participate in sports but rather some end result. Anyone who exerts himself is active. We then say he is "busy." And to be "busy" is to be engaged in "business."

What constitutes passivity in this view? If we produce no visible results, no palpable achievement, then we have been passive. Let me cite an obvious example: Someone sits still looking out into the landscape, just sits there for five minutes, half an hour, maybe even an hour. He does nothing but look. Because he is not taking any pictures but is simply immersing himself in what his eyes are perceiving, we might regard him as strange and would not be at all inclined to grace his "contemplativeness" with the name of activity. Or consider someone who meditates (though in our Western culture the sight of someone meditating is rare indeed). He is attempting to become aware of himself, of his own feelings, his moods, his inner state of being. If he meditates regularly and systematically, he may spend hours at it. Anyone who understands nothing of meditation would consider that meditator a passive person. He is not doing anything. Perhaps his whole effort is aimed at driving every last thought out of his mind, thinking about nothing, and simply being. That may strike you as peculiar. Try it sometime, just for two minutes, and you'll see how difficult it is, how something or other will keep popping into your head, how your mind will drift to every last bit of trivia under the sun, how defenseless you are against those thoughts because we find it nearly intolerable to sit still and turn off our thoughts.

For great cultures in India and China that kind of meditation is vitally important. Unfortunately that is not the case with us, because, ambition-ridden as we are, we think everything we do has to have a purpose, to achieve something, to produce a result. But if you try to forget about results for once, if you can concentrate and bring enough patience to this exercise, you may find the "idleness" very refreshing indeed.

All I have meant to suggest here is that our modern usage labels behavior that produces visible results activity, while passivity appears to be pointless. It is behavior in which we detect no output of energy. That we see activity and passivity that way has to do with the issue of how and what we consume. If we consume the superfluous things our "bad affluence" supplies us with, what appears to be activity on our part is really passivity. What kind of creative activity, of "good affluence," of richness, of resistance can we imagine that would allow us to be more than mere consumers?

7

Ennui in Modern Society

Let's reflect for a moment on the classic definitions of activity and passivity we find in Aristotle, Spinoza, Goethe, Marx, and many other thinkers of the Western world over the last two thousand years. *Activity* is understood as something that brings the powers inherent in people to expression, that helps give birth, that brings to life both our physical and emotional, both our intellectual and artistic capacities. Perhaps some of you will not quite understand what I mean when I speak of powers inherent in people, for we are accustomed to thinking of power and energy as residing in machines, not in people. And whatever powers human beings do possess are channeled primarily into inventing and operating machines. As we marvel more and more over the power of machines, we understand less and less of the wonderful powers of human beings. We no longer quite believe those lines from Sophocles' *Antigone:* "Numberless are the world's wonders, but none/ More wonderful than man." A rocket that can fly to the moon seems far more wonderful to us than a mere human being. And in a certain sense we feel that in our modern inventions we have created things more marvelous than God did when he created man.

We have to reorient our thinking if we mean to focus our attention on human consciousness and on the development of the vast potential human beings have. We possess not only the ability to speak and to think but also a capacity for ever deeper insight, for ever greater maturity, a capacity for love and for artistic expression. All those things are potentially present in us, waiting to be developed. Activity, being active in the way that the authors I have named understand it, means just that: the bringing out, the manifesting of those powers that human beings have but that usually remain hidden or suppressed.

I'd like to read you some lines from Karl Marx here. You will quickly realize that this is a very different Marx from the one you usually encounter at the university, in the media, or in propaganda issued by either the Left or the Right. This quotation is from the Economic-Philosophical Manuscripts (MEGA, I,3, p. 149): "If you take as your point of departure the human being as human being and his relationship to the world as a human one, then you can give only love in return for love, trust in return for trust, etc. . . . If you want to influence other people, then you have to be a person who genuinely stimulates and challenges others. Each of your relationships with people—and with nature—has to be a specific expression of your own true, individual life appropriate to the object of your intentions. If you love without awakening love in return, that is, if your love as love does not produce a loving response, if the expression of your being as a loving person does not make you loved, then your love is powerless and brings unhappiness."

It is clear that Marx speaks of loving here as a kind of activity. It rarely occurs to modern man that he can create anything through love. His usual and almost exclusive concern is to be loved, not to emanate love himself, not to awaken love in others through his love for them and so to create something new, something that had not existed in the world before. That is why he thinks that being loved is purely a matter of chance or something you can make happen by buying all sorts of things that will supposedly make you lovable, everything from the right mouthwash to an elegant suit or an expensive car. Now, just what the right mouthwash or the right suit will do for you I really can't say. But I do have to acknowledge as an unfortunate fact that many men are loved for their sporty cars. And here we have to add, of course, that many men are fonder of their cars than they are of their wives. At any rate, both partners to such an arrangement often seem quite content, but after a while they will become bored with each other and possibly even hate each other, because they have both been deceived or will at least feel deceived. They thought they were loved, but in reality all they have done is pretend at love. They have not practiced active love.

Similarly, when we say, in the classic sense of the word, that someone is *passive,* we do not mean that he sits still, reflects, meditates, or looks at the natural world; we mean instead that he is driven by forces he does not control, that he cannot act but can only react.

On the subject of reaction we should not forget, of course, that most of our activity consists of reacting to stimuli, to situations, which, because we are familiar with them, evoke a given response from us when we perceive the appropriate signal. Because the dog in Pavlov's experiment had learned to associate food with the sound of a bell, he developed an appetite whenever he heard the bell. In running for his food dish, he was very "active." But that activity was nothing but a reaction to a stimulus. The dog functioned like a machine. Behaviorism concerns itself with processes of this very kind: Man is a reactive being. Present him with a stimulus, and he will promptly react to it. We can experiment in the same way with rats, with mice, with monkeys, with human beings, even with cats, though with cats things don't always go as they're supposed to. Human beings—alas!—are the most susceptible to that approach. Behaviorism assumes that all human behavior is essentially governed by the principle of rewards and punishments. Reward and punishment are the two great stimuli, and a human being will presumably react to them the way any other animal does. He will learn to do the things for which he is rewarded and not to do the ones for which there is a threat of punishment. He doesn't necessarily have to be punished; the threat of punishment alone suffices. Every now and then, of course, a few people do indeed have to be punished so that the threat of punishment does not become an empty threat.

Now let's look at what it means to be "driven." Take a drunken person, for example. He may well be very "active." He yells and waves his arms around. Or think of someone in that psychotic state that we describe as "manic." Such a person is hyperactive; he thinks he can help the whole world; he talks a blue streak, sends telegrams, gets things moving. He appears to be prodigiously active. But we know that in the first case the motor behind the activity is alcohol; in the manic patient, it is some electrochemical malfunction in the brain. The external manifestations in both cases, though, appear to be those of extreme activity.

"Activity" that is either a mere reaction to a stimulus or a "driveness" or compulsion manifested as passion is, in reality, passivity, no matter how great a stir it may make. Our words "passion" and "passive" derive from *passio* and *passivus* respectively, both of which stem in turn from the Latin verb meaning "to suffer." So if we say of someone that he is a very passionate person, we are paying him a rather dubious compliment. The philosopher Schleiermacher once said: *Eifersucht ist eine Leidenschaft, die mit Eifer sucht, was Leiden schafft* (Jealousy is a passion that eagerly pursues what brings about suffering). That is true not only of jealousy but of any passion that takes on a compulsive character: ambition, greed, the lust for power, gluttony. All addictions are passions that create suffering. They are forms of passivity. "Passion" has taken on a wider range of meaning in our modern usage and so has lost the clarity it once had. I will not go into the reasons for that here.

Now if you take a close look at the activity of people who merely react or who act compulsively, people who are therefore passive in the classical sense, you will notice that their reactions never take a new direction. Their reactions are always the same. The same stimulus will always produce the same reaction. You can predict with certainty what will happen each time. Everything can be calculated. There is no individuality in evidence here; no powers of thought come into play; everything seems to be programmed: the same stimulus, the same effect. We see the same thing happening that we can observe with rats in a laboratory. Since behaviorism sees the human being primarily as a mechanism, it makes similar assumptions about him: A certain stimulus will evoke a certain response. The study and exploration of that phenomenon and the formulation of prescriptions based on it is what the behaviorists call science. Perhaps it is a science, but it is not a humane one, for a living human being never reacts twice in precisely the same way. At each moment he is a different person. And though he may never be a totally different person, he is at least never exactly the same. Heraclites expressed the same idea when he said, "It is impossible to wade into the same river twice." The reason is, of course, that the river is constantly flowing. I would say that behavioral psychology may be a science, but it is not a science of man. It is rather a science of alienated man conducted with alienated methods by alienated researchers. It may be capable of illuminating certain aspects of human nature, but it does not touch on what is vital, on what is specifically human about human beings.

I'd like to give you an example illustrating the difference between activity and passivity, one that made a great impact on industrial psychology in America. The Western Electric Company commissioned Professor Elton Mayo to find out how the productivity of unskilled female workers in its Hawthorne plant in Chicago could be increased. Mayo proceeded on the assumption that the workers would probably be more productive if they were given a ten-minute break in the morning and perhaps another ten-minute coffee break in the afternoon, and so on. Those unskilled workers had the very monotonous task of winding coils for electromagnets. Their work required neither skill nor exertion; it was the most passive, dreary work imaginable. Elton Mayo explained his experiment to the workers and then proceeded to give them a coffee break in the afternoon. Productivity increased immediately. Everyone was, of course, delighted to see how well the idea worked. Then Mayo went a step further and gave the workers a break in the morning, too, and productivity increased once again. Still further improvements in working conditions brought even greater gains in productivity, and so it seemed that Mayo's theory had been proved conclusively.

Any ordinary professor would have broken off his experiment at that point and advised Western Electric's management to sacrifice twenty minutes of work time a day in the interests of increased production. Not so Elton Mayo, who was quite an ingenious fellow. He was wondering what would happen if he withdrew the amenities he had granted the workers. So he canceled the afternoon coffee break—and production continued to increase. Then he took away the morning break, too. Another increase in production. And so on and so forth. At that point some professors might have shrugged their shoulders and declared the experiment invalid. But in this case it suddenly dawned on Mayo that those unskilled workers had, for the first time in their lives, developed an interest in what they were doing. The winding of coils remained as monotonous as it had ever been, but Mayo had explained his experiment to the workers and drawn them into it. They felt that they were working in a meaningful context, that they were contributing something that profited not only an anonymous management but the entire work force as well. Mayo was thus able to demonstrate that it was this unexpected interest, this sense of participation and not the morning and afternoon coffee breaks, that had increased production. The experiment inspired a new approach to industrial psychology: The *interest* people brought to their work appeared to have a greater bearing on their productivity than did breaks, pay increases, or any other amenities. I'll be coming back to this point later on, but for now all I wanted to do was emphasize the crucial difference between activity and passivity. As long as the Western Electric workers had no interest in their jobs, they remained passive. But the minute they were given a part in the experiment, they felt that they were making a real contribution; they became active and developed an entirely different attitude toward their work.

Take another, simpler example. Imagine a tourist—with a camera, of course—who arrives somewhere and finds a mountain, a lake, a castle, or an art exhibit in front of him. He cannot really take in what he sees, because he is too preoccupied with the photograph he will make of it. For him the only relevant reality is the one he can record on film and take possession of, not the one that is actually before him. The second step, the picture, comes before the first, the act of seeing itself. Once he has his picture he can show it to his friends as if to suggest that he himself created this recorded segment of the world, or ten years later he can recall where he was at the time. But in either case the photograph, the artificial perception, has crowded out the original one. Many tourists don't even bother to look first. They just grab for their cameras. A good photographer will first try to capture for himself what he will later try to capture with the camera. He will try to relate to what it is he wants to photograph. That preliminary seeing is a kind of activity. The difference between those two ways of seeing cannot be measured in a laboratory, but the expressions on people's faces will give you a clue to it: Someone who has seen something beautiful will register his pleasure in his face. He may then choose to photograph or not to photograph what he has seen. There are people (though their number is few) who deliberately choose not to take photographs because they feel pictures interfere with their memories. With a picture, your recollection is limited to what the picture shows you. But if you try to recall a landscape without the aid of a picture, you will find the landscape reborn within you. The scene returns, and it is as vivid to your mind's eye as it was in reality. It is not a mere schematic memory, like a word you may recall. You recreate that landscape for yourself; it is you who produce the scene you see. This kind of activity refreshes, brightens, and strengthens our vital energies. Passivity, by contrast, deadens and depresses us and may even fill us with hate.

Imagine for a moment that you have been invited to a party. You already know what this or that person will say to you, what you will say in reply, and what the other will say back. What everyone will say is clear and predictable, as if you were in a world of machines. Everyone has his or her opinion, his or her view. Nothing happens, and when you go home you are dead tired, weary to the bone. Yet while you were at the party, you probably gave the impression of being lively and active. You chatted away, just as your partners in conversation chatted away at you. You may even have become excited. But for all that your exchanges remained passive. You and your partners did nothing but roll your old selves out again and again. The pattern of stimulus and response held sway like an old, worn-out record. Nothing new emerged. Boredom triumphed.

Now it's a remarkable phenomenon in our culture that people do not fully acknowledge or—perhaps we should say—are not fully conscious of what a grave affliction boredom is. Take someone in solitary confinement or, to use a less drastic example, take someone who simply doesn't know what to do with himself for whatever reason. Unless such a person has the resources within himself to engage in some vital activity, to produce something, or to call his intellectual powers into play, then he will perceive his boredom as a burden, an encumbrance, a paralysis that he will not be able to explain by himself. Boredom is one of the worst forms of torture. It is a very modern phenomenon, and it is spreading rapidly. A person who is at the mercy of his boredom and unable to defend himself against it will feel severely depressed. You may feel moved to ask here why most people don't notice how grave a malady boredom is and how much suffering it causes us. I think the answer is quite simple. We produce today so many things that people can take to help them cope with their boredom. We can temporarily sweep our boredom under the rug by taking a tranquilizer or drinking or going to one cocktail party after another or fighting with our wives or turning to the media for amusement or devoting ourselves to sexual activity. Much of what we do is an attempt to keep ourselves from fully acknowledging our boredom. But don't forget that uneasy feeling that often overcomes you when you've watched a stupid movie or repressed your boredom some other way. Remember the hangover that hits you when you realize that what you did for diversion actually bored you to death and that you haven't made use of your time but have killed it. Another remarkable thing about our culture is that we will go to any lengths to save time, but once we have saved it we kill it because we can't think of anything better to do with it.

Manufactured Needs

It is a commonly held view—not only among laymen but also among many scientists—that human beings are machines that function in accordance with certain physiological requirements. They experience hunger and thirst; they have to sleep; they need sex, and so on. The physiological or biological needs have to be met. If they are not, people will become neurotic or, if they don't eat, for example, they will die. If those needs are met, however, then everything is just fine. Now the only trouble with that view is that it's wrong. It can happen that all a person's physiological and biological needs are met but he is still not satisfied, still is not at peace with himself. Indeed, he may be psychically quite ill even though he seems to have everything he needs. What he lacks is an animating impulse that would make him active.

Let me give you a few brief examples of what I mean. In recent years some interesting experiments have been conducted in which people have been deprived of all stimuli. They have been placed in complete isolation in a small space where the temperature and illumination remain constant. Their food is shoved in to them through a hatchway. All their needs are met, but there are no stimuli. The conditions are comparable, say, to those a fetus experiences in the womb. After a few days' exposure to this kind of experiment, people begin to develop serious pathological tendencies, often schizophrenic ones. Although their physiological needs are satisfied, this state of passivity is psychologically pathogenic and can lead to insanity. What is a normal situation for a fetus (although even a fetus is not as fully deprived of stimuli as the subjects in those experiments are) produces illness in an adult.

In still other experiments, people have been prevented from dreaming. It is possible to do this because we know that very rapid eye movements accompany dreaming. If an experimenter wakes a subject when he sees rapid eye movements, he can keep that individual from dreaming. People subjected to this experiment, too, developed serious symptoms of illness. This suggests that dreaming is a psychic necessity. Even when we are asleep, we remain mentally and psychologically active. If we are kept from that activity, we become ill.

The animal psychologist Harlow found in his experiments with monkeys that primates could maintain their interest in a complicated experiment for ten hours at a time. They worked persistently at taking apart a complex structure and stuck patiently at their task. No rewards were offered or punishments inflicted. Because Harlow did not make any use of the stimulus–response mechanism, it was clear that the animals persisted in their work out of sheer interest in it. Animals, too, especially the primates, can develop high levels of interest and are not motivated exclusively by the promise of food or the fear of punishment.

Let me mention still another example. Human beings were producing art as long ago as 30,000 years. We are inclined to belittle that work today by saying it served purely magical ends. Think of the incredibly beautiful and graceful renderings of animals we find in cave paintings. The motivation for those paintings was presumably to ensure success in the hunt. That may well be, but does that explain their beauty? The needs of magic could have been met with far less artistic painting and decorating of caves and vases. The beauty that we can still perceive and enjoy today was an added extra. In other words, people have other interests that go beyond the practical, the functional, the object as tool or utensil. They want to be active in a creative way; they want to give shape to things, to develop powers latent in themselves.

The German psychologist Karl Buehler has coined the very apt phrase "the delight of function" to suggest the joy that activity can bring with it. People enjoy functioning not because they need this thing or that thing but because the act of making something, the utilization of their own capacities, itself is a pleasurable experience. That point has, of course, an important bearing on education. A brilliant Italian teacher, Maria Montessori, realized that children can be *trained* with the old system of rewards and punishments, but they cannot be *educated* with it. Numerous studies designed to test that idea have confirmed that people do indeed learn better when what they do is itself inherently satisfying.

I believe a human being is fully himself only when he expresses himself, when he makes use of the powers within him. If he cannot do that, if his life consists only of possessing and using rather than being, then he degenerates; he becomes a thing; his life becomes pointless. It becomes a form of suffering. Real joy comes with real activity, and real activity involves the utilization and cultivation of human powers. We should not forget that exerting our minds encourages the growth of brain cells. That is a fact supported by physiological evidence. Indeed, the growth of the brain can even be weighed and is analogous to the strengthening of muscles of which we make increased demands. If we never subject our muscles to more stress than they are accustomed to, they will remain at the stage of development they have attained, but they will never come near what they are potentially capable of.

Now I would like to introduce some social and economic considerations into our discussion of affluence. We can distinguish a few major phases in human history. Perhaps we should begin by noting that the phase in which man evolved from the apes was a very long one extending over a few hundred thousand years. There was no single step or moment that marked the completion of that development. It was a long process in which quantitative factors underwent a very gradual transformation into qualitative ones. The evolutionary process that produced the precursor of modern man was more or less complete only 60,000 years ago; and *Homo sapiens,* a creature who is just like us today, first appeared about 40,000 years ago. Our beginnings, then, go back only a very short time.

What is it that distinguishes man from the animals? It is not his upright posture. That was present in the apes long before the brain began to develop. Nor is it the use of tools. It is something altogether new, a previously unknown quality: self-awareness. Animals, too, have awareness. They are aware of objects; they know this is one thing and that another. But when the human being as such was born he had a new and different consciousness, a consciousness of himself; he knew that he existed and that he was something different, something apart from nature, apart from other people, too. He experienced himself. He was aware that he thought and felt. As far as we know, there is nothing analogous to this anywhere else in the animal kingdom. That is the specific quality that makes human beings human.

From the moment that man was born as what we would call a full human being he lived for roughly 30,000 years in a situation of prevailing hardship, of perpetual shortage. He lived by hunting animals and by gathering foodstuffs that he could use but had not cultivated. Life in that period was marked by poverty and need. But then came a great revolution that is sometimes called the Neolithic evolution. That revolution occurred about 10,000 years ago. Man began to produce, to create material goods. He no longer lived only from what he happened to find or from the yield of the hunt but became a farmer or herdsman. He produced more than he needed at the moment, using his foresight, his intelligence, and his skills to make what he needed himself.

The first farmers with their simple plows may strike us today as very primitive, but they were the first people to escape from total dependence on the whims of nature, to which all men before had been subject, and to start using their brains, imaginations, and energies to influence the world and create more hospitable environments for themselves. They planned; they provided for the future; they created, for the first time, a relative affluence. They soon left primitive methods of agriculture and animal husbandry behind. They developed culture; they developed cities; and a second era followed quickly on the heels of the first: an era characterized by relative affluence. By "relative affluence" I mean a state in which the earlier poverty and need had been overcome but in which the new affluence was too confined to let everyone partake of it. The minority that controlled society and accumulated increasing power kept the best of everything for itself, leaving only the left-overs for the majority. The table was not set for everyone. Affluence was not available to all. Thus, though we may be oversimplifying for the sake of brevity, we can speak of the relative affluence (or relative poverty) that has been the rule since the beginning of the Neolithic revolution and that is still, to some measure, the rule today.

Relative affluence is a two-edged sword. On the one hand, people were able to develop cultures. They had the material base they needed to build buildings, organize states, support philosophers, and so forth. But on the other hand, the consequence of relative poverty was that a small group had to exploit a large one. Without the majority, that economy could not have flourished. The warring impulse is not, as many people like to claim, rooted in human instinct, in man's natural drive to destroy. War had its beginnings in the Neolithic period from the moment when there were things worth taking away from someone else and when people had established their communal life in such a way that they could invent war as an institution and use it to attack others who had something they wanted. We usually have complicated reasons on hand to explain why we go to war. "We were threatened!" we say, and that is supposed to justify a war. The real motivations behind wars are usually pathetically transparent.

So we have relative affluence, this accomplishment of the Neolithic period, to thank for culture on the one hand and for war and the exploitation of man by man on the other. Ever since that period human beings have lived more or less in a zoo. Accordingly, the entire field of psychology, which is based on the observation of human beings, can be compared with that stage in ethology when all of our knowledge of animals was based on observations made in zoos and not in the wild. It has become particularly clear to psychologists that animals in zoos behave very differently from animals in the wild. Solly Zuckerman observed that the sacred baboons in the London Zoo in Regents Park were incredibly aggressive. He assumed at first that the trait lay in the nature of those particular primates. But when other scientists observed those baboons in the wild, they found them not very aggressive at all. Imprisonment, boredom, the limitations on freedom—all these things encouraged the development of an aggression that was absent in natural conditions.

My point is simply that both man and animal behave differently when they are held captive from the way they do when they are free. But then the first industrial revolution brought about a great change in the human situation, a change that had its beginnings as far back as the Renaissance but has come to a head in our century: All of a sudden *mechanical* energy took the place of *natural* energy, that is, energy supplied by animals and human beings. Now machines supplied the power that had formerly been supplied by living beings. And at the same time a new hope arose. If that energy could be harnessed, then everyone, not just a minority, could enjoy the fruits of affluence.

On the heels of the first revolution followed another that has been called the second industrial revolution. In this revolution machines replace not only human *energy* but also human *thought.* I am referring here to the science of cybernetics and to the machines that have themselves assumed control of other machines and of the production process. Cybernetics has increased and continues to increase production possibilities to such a massive degree that we can realistically foresee a time—assuming that a war does not break out first or that humanity is not decimated by hunger or epidemics—when the new production methods will provide absolute affluence. At that point no one will be poor or in need any more; everyone will know affluence. Human life will not be cluttered with the superfluous but will be marked by a positive abundance that frees people from the fear of hunger, the fear of violence.

Our modern society has developed still another thing that never existed before. It produces not only goods but also needs. What do I mean by that? People have always had needs. They have had to eat and drink. They have wanted to live in attractive homes, and so forth. But if you look around you today you will note the ever increasing importance that advertising and packaging have acquired. It is rare for desires to arise within people any more; desires are awakened and cultivated from without. Even someone who is well off will feel poor when confronted with the plethora of goods the advertisers want him to want. There is no doubt whatsoever that industry will succeed in creating needs that it will then set about satisfying, indeed, will have to satisfy if it means to stay alive in the present system, for in that system the production of a profit is the test of viability. Our present economic system is based on maximum production and maximum consumption. The nineteenth-century economy was still based on the idea of maximizing savings. Our grandparents considered it a vice to buy something you didn't have the money to pay for. Today that has become a virtue. And, conversely, anyone without such artificial needs, anyone who does not buy on credit, anyone who buys only what he truly needs borders on the politically suspect; he is a peculiar sort. People who don't own television sets stand out. They are obviously not quite normal. Where will this all lead us? I can tell you. The unlimited increase of consumption produces a type of person who is devoted to an ideal, indeed, to what is almost a new religion, the religion of the Big Rock Candy Mountain. If we ask ourselves how modern man envisions paradise, we are probably correct in saying that, unlike the Mohammedans, he does not expect to find himself surrounded by beautiful women there (a decidedly male view of paradise anyway). His vision is of an immense department store where everything is available and where he will always have money enough to buy not only everything he wants but also just a little bit more than his neighbor. That is part of the syndrome: His sense of self-worth is based on how much he has. And if he wants to be the best he has to have the most.

The question of where to call a halt founders in the almost frenzied rounds of production and consumption, and even though most people in this economic system have much more than they can use, they still feel poor because they cannot keep up with the pace of production or the mass of goods produced. This situation promotes passivity as well as envy and greed and, ultimately, a sense of inner weakness, of powerlessness, of inferiority. A person's sense of self comes to be based solely on what he *has*, not on what he *is*.

The Crisis of the Patriarchal Order

As we have seen, orienting our lives to consumption creates a climate of superfluity and ennui. The problem is closely related to a crisis that is affecting the entire Western world now but mostly goes unrecognized, because more attention is given to its symptoms than to its underlying causes. What I have in mind here is the crisis of our patriarchal, authoritarian social structure.

What exactly is that structure? Let me begin my explanation by harking back to one of the greatest thinkers of the nineteenth century, the Swiss scholar Johann Jakob Bachofen, who was the first to demonstrate systematically that societies are based on one of two completely different structural principles: a gynecocratic, matriarchal one or a patriarchal one. What is the difference between them?

In patriarchal society as we know it from the Old Testament and from the Romans and as we still have it today, the father owns and rules the family. When I use the word "own" here I mean it quite literally; for originally, in primitive patriarchal law, wives and children were as much the property of the *pater familias* as slaves or cattle were. He could do with them what he wished. If we think of today's youth, it may seem that we have come a long way from that ancient law. But we should not overlook the fact that the patriarchal principle has been in force in the Western world, in more or less drastic form, for about 4,000 years.

In a matriarchal society, things are just the other way around. The person who is most respected, who is regarded as the undisputed head of the family, and of whom no one would dream of referring to as a "ruler" is the mother, the maternal figure. There is a vast difference between paternal love and maternal love, and that difference is of great importance. Paternal love is by its very nature always a conditional love. Children have to earn it by meeting certain requirements. Now please don't misunderstand me. When I speak of paternal love, I don't mean the love of Father X or Father Y; I mean paternal love in the abstract. Max Weber would have spoken of an "ideal type." The father loves that son best who best fulfills the father's expectations and demands. That son is then the most likely to become his father's successor and heir. In a patriarchal family structure there is usually a favorite son, ordinarily—but not necessarily—the eldest. If you look back in the Old Testament, you'll find that there is always a favorite son there. His father grants him a special status; he is the "chosen one." He pleases his father because he obeys him.

Things are just the opposite in a matriarchal structure. A mother loves all her children equally. They are all, without exception, the

21

fruit of her womb, and they all need her care. If mothers nursed only those of their infants who pleased them and obeyed them, then most children would die. As you know, an infant hardly ever does what its mother would like it to do. If mothers were guided by paternal love, that would be the biological, physiological end of the human race. A mother loves her child because it is her child, and that is why no hierarchies develop in matriarchal societies. There is instead the same love available to all who need care and affection.

What I have just presented here is a brief summary of Bachofen's ideas. In a patriarchal society, the ruling principles are the state, the law, the abstract. In a matriarchal one, they are the natural bonds that draw people together. They do not have to be thought up and put into practice. They are natural bonds that are simply there. If you want to take the time to read Sophocles' *Antigone,* you'll find there everything I've been trying to tell you here but in a much fuller and more interesting form. The play chronicles a battle between the patriarchal principle, embodied by Creon, and the matriarchal principle, represented by Antigone. For Creon, the law of the state stands supreme, and whoever defies that law has to die. Antigone, however, follows the law of blood ties, of humanity, of sympathy, and no one can violate this highest of all laws. The play ends with the defeat of the principle we would call fascistic today. Creon is portrayed as a typically fascist leader who believes in nothing but power and in a state to which the individual has to subordinate himself totally.

We mustn't fail to mention religion in this context. Ever since the Old Testament, the religion of the Western world has been patriarchal. God is depicted as a great authority we should all obey. In Buddhism, however, to mention only one example of another major religion, that authoritarian figure is not present. The view of the conscience as an internalized authority is an inevitable outgrowth of patriarchal society. What Freud meant when he spoke of the superego was our internalizing of paternal commands and prohibitions. My father no longer has to tell me, "Don't do that!" to keep me from doing something. I have absorbed my father into myself. The "father inside me" commands and prohibits. But the force of the command or prohibition still goes back to paternal authority. Freud's description of conscience in a patriarchal society is completely correct, but he is mistaken in regarding that kind of conscience as conscience *per se* and in failing to see conscience in a societal context. For if we look at nonpatriarchal societies, we find quite different forms of conscience. I cannot and do not want to go into this issue in any detail here, but I do at least want to mention that there is a humanistic conscience that stands in direct opposition to the authoritarian one. A humanistic conscience is rooted in the individual himself and communicates to him what is good and beneficial for him, for his development, for his growth. That voice often speaks very softly, and we are good at ignoring it. But in the realm of physiology as well as in that of psychology researchers have found signs of what we might call a "health conscience," a sense for what is good for us; and if people listen to that voice inside them, they will not obey the voice of some external authority. Our own internal voices guide us in directions that are compatible with the physical and psychic potential of our particular organisms. Those voices tell us: You're on the right track here; you're on the wrong one there.

We have to keep all this in mind when we consider the present crisis of the patriarchal, authoritarian order, a crisis that confronts us with a remarkable situation. In the Western world, we are experiencing the disintegration of traditional values. And as I have already suggested, that disintegration, that crisis, is in some way linked to our problem of affluence. Let me try to make this clearer. The more deprivation a person has to put up with, the more obedient he has to be so that he will not rebel against the deprivation imposed on him. He is told that the deprivation he is forced to endure is meaningful and inevitable, something that God or the state or the law—or whoever—has to demand of him. If it were not for unquestioning obedience, it might occur to people that they don't feel like being deprived any longer. And that would, of course, be extremely dangerous for any social order in which deprivation and obedience are indispensable structural elements. Society as we know it could not exist any more if psychological mechanisms and social institutions had not firmly implanted obedience and the acceptance of deprivation as widespread attitudes in it. But if affluence increases, the belief that we have to be obedient and accept deprivation will necessarily lose its force. Why should we submit to an authority that asks us to obey and suffer deprivation? We can have just about anything we want in any case. That is one reason for the present crisis.

Another no doubt lies in the new methods of production. In the first industrial revolution, that is, throughout the nineteenth century and well into the twentieth, when old-fashioned machines were in use, it was essential for the worker to obey, because his work was the only thing that kept his family from starving. Some of that forced obedience is still with us, but that is changing rapidly as production shifts more and more away from outmoded mechanical technologies and toward modern cybernetic ones. With the new technology, the form of authoritarian obedience that was needed in the previous century is no longer necessary. Today work is characterized by team effort, and people are working with machines that, for the most part, correct their mistakes themselves. The old obedience has been replaced with a kind of discipline that does not require subordination. Workers play with cybernetic machines almost as one would at chess. That is surely something of an exaggeration, but a fundamental change in our attitude toward machinery has taken place. The old relationship of supervisor and worker is becoming less common; a style characterized by cooperation and interdependence is gaining ground. Let me add as an aside that the new working climate is not so idyllic, not so positive, as is sometimes claimed or as it may appear in what I have just said here. I do not mean to claim that modern production methods have put an end to alienation and helped us achieve independence. All I have wanted to do here is call attention to important departures from the past.

Still another reason for the crisis of the patriarchal, authoritarian order is the fact of political revolution. Starting with the French Revolution we have experienced a whole series of revolutions, none of which has fulfilled its promises and goals, but all of which, however, have undermined the old order and called authoritarian structures into question. We have witnessed the slow but sure demise of the blind obedience without which the feudal system could not have maintained itself. The very fact of a revolution that is even partially successful, a revolution that is not a total failure, demonstrates that disobedience can be victorious.

In authoritarian morality there is only one sin, which is disobedience, and there is only one virtue, which is obedience. No one will admit that outright—except perhaps in reactionary circles—but in reality the underlying conviction of our educational system and of our whole system of values is that disobedience is the root of all evil.

Take the Old Testament, for example. What Adam and Eve did was not in itself bad. On the contrary, their eating of the tree of knowledge of good and evil was what made the development of humankind possible. But they were disobedient, and the tradition has interpreted that disobedience as original sin. And in a patriarchal society disobedience is in fact original sin. But now that the patriarchal order has been called into doubt, now that it is in a state of crisis and collapse, the concept of sin itself has become altogether questionable. We shall be coming back to this point later.

Along with the revolution of the middle class and the revolution of the workers we have to mention another very important one: the feminist revolution. Even though that revolution may assume some rather bizarre forms now and then, it has made remarkable advances. Women, like children, used to be regarded as objects, as the property of their husbands. That has changed. They may still be at a disadvantage in a man's world, receiving less pay, for example, than a man does for the same work; but their overall position, their consciousness, is considerably stronger than it was. And all the signs would seem to indicate that the women's revolution will go forward, just as the revolution of children and young people will. They will continue to define, articulate, and stand up for their own rights.

And now let me mention the last and what I think to be the most important reason for the crisis of patriarchal society. Ever since the middle of this century many people, but primarily young people, have come to the conclusion that our society is incompetent. Now you may object that we have great achievements to our credit and that our technology has made unheard-of advances. But that is only one side of the story. The other side is that this society has proved itself incapable of preventing two great wars and many smaller ones. It has not only allowed but actually promoted developments that are leading us toward the suicide of humankind. Never before in our history have we been faced with so much potential for destruction as we are today. That fact points to a horrendous incompetence that no technological perfection can gloss over.

When a society that is affluent enough to afford visits to the moon is unable to face and reduce the danger of total annihilation, then—like it or not—that society will have to accept the label of incompetent. It is incompetent, too, in the face of the environmental degradation that threatens all life. Famine is in store for India and Africa, for all the nonindustrialized nations of the world, but our only response is a few speeches and empty gestures. We go on merrily in our extravagant ways as if we lacked the intelligence to see the consequences of those ways. That demonstrates a lack of competence. It has shaken the younger generation's trust in us, and with good reason. And so I feel that in spite of all the merits of our success-oriented society this lack of competence in dealing with our most urgent problems has done much to destroy faith in the structure and effectiveness of the patriarchal, authoritarian order.

Before we take a closer look at the consequences of this crisis I would like to stress here that even in the Western world we have only a partially affluent society. In the United States almost 40 percent of the population lives below the poverty line. There are, in reality, two classes: one that lives in affluence and another whose poverty everyone else would just as soon not acknowledge. In Lincoln's time the great social distinction was between freedom and slavery; today it is between superfluous affluence and poverty.

Everything I have said here about *Homo consumens* does not hold true for people living in poverty, fascinated though they may be by the idea that those who enjoy luxury are leading a paradisiacal life. The poor are only extras who help fill up the wide screens the rich look at for amusement. The same is true for minorities; in the United States it is especially true for nonwhites. But above and beyond that it is true throughout the whole world. It is true for those two-thirds of all humanity who have never profited from the patriarchal, authoritarian social order, true for the Indians, the Chinese, the Africans, and so on. If we are to draw an accurate picture of the relationship between authoritarian and nonauthoritarian populations, we have to realize that though the affluent society may continue to dominate in the world today, it is being confronted not only with totally different traditions but also with new forces that we have already begun to feel and will continue to feel.

The Fiasco of Religion

Although most people if asked in a poll would say they believe in God, and though church attendance still remains high and confessions of atheism are relatively rare, it is still perfectly clear that the crisis in patriarchal society has also had a negative effect on religion. Theologians themselves have realized this and have spoken quite openly about the anguish religion as we know it is currently going through. The development began centuries ago, but the closer we come to the present, the greater its rate of acceleration has been.

Because religion fulfills a double function, its collapse leaves us with a double loss. Our religion, based primarily on the Judeo-Christian tradition, provides us with both an explanation of the natural world and moral principles—an ethic. Those two functions have nothing to do with each other, for how you explain the natural world is one thing, and what moral principles and values you have is quite another. But the two functions were not originally separated, and there are a number of reasons why they were not. First of all, the idea that the world was created by a god who incorporated in himself the highest intelligence, wisdom, and power was a plausible, indeed, a rational hypothesis. And even if you are a convinced Darwinist who sees the development of the world and of man as a consequence of natural selection or mutation, you may still feel that the postulation of God the Creator is much easier to understand and accept than the rather complex alternative; for evolutionary theory claims that man in his present form is the product of certain principles that went into effect hundreds of millions of years ago and that are to some degree subject to pure chance or, at best, to the laws of natural selection. Darwin's explanation of the natural world seems altogether logical and plausible, but despite that it remains alien to our minds.

Man has always had a need, even in his earliest, most primitive stages, to form a picture of the world and of its creation. One version of the creation that goes far back in time claims that human beings were made out of the blood that flowed from someone who had been killed. Not *everyone* was made of that blood, however. Only the brave were. Cowards and women were made from the flesh of the two legs. That is an ancient version of the theory that Konrad Lorenz has put forward, namely, that human beings have an inborn instinct to kill, a blood lust. It was nice, of course, of the people who believed in the myth to exempt women from that blood lust, but it was not so nice of them then to throw women in with the cowards. Things have not changed much even today. According to the prejudices of patriarchal society, women have less conscience, are more vain and cowardly, and are less realistic than men. Now all those claims are notoriously false. In many cases the shoe could easily be put on the other foot. Most women know what a pathetic figure a man can cut when he is sick. He is much more given to self-pity and much less secure in himself than a woman. But no one admits that for fear of destroying the myth. We see the same thing happening here that we see in racial stereotypes. What men say about women has no more basis in fact than what the whites say about the blacks. Even Freud claimed that women had less conscience than men. Now I find it hard to imagine how anybody could have less conscience than men. What those claims are, of course, is nothing more than propaganda about the inferiority of an enemy. That kind of propaganda turns up whenever one group dominates another and discourages rebellion by holding the self-confidence of the dominated group down to an absolute minimum.

That is by way of a little footnote to one of the functions of religion I mentioned above, to wit, an explanation of the natural world. Everything went along just fine until Darwin, but what we learned from him was that if we looked at the creation of the world and of man from a rational and scientific point of view we could dispense with the idea of God and explain those phenomena by the laws of evolution. As I said, it is easier for the layman to grasp the idea of God, but for science after Darwin the creation was no longer a mystery. In the light of the theory of evolution, "God" was reduced to a working hypothesis and the story of the creation of the world and of man to a myth, a poem, a symbol, which clearly expressed something but could no longer be regarded as scientific truth.

Once the religious explanation of the natural world lost its power to convince, religion lost one leg, as it were. All that remained for it to stand on was the propagation of moral postulates. "Love thy neighbor," the Old Testament says. "Love the stranger." The New Testament says, "Love your enemies" and "Go and sell that thou hast, and give to the poor." How can anyone who takes those instructions seriously be successful in modern society? Anyone who follows those precepts is a fool. He'll fall behind, not get ahead. We preach the moral precepts of the Bible but don't practice them. We run on two separate tracks. Altruism is praised; we're supposed to have love for our neighbors. But at the same time the pressure to succeed keeps us from practicing those virtues.

I have to add a qualifying note here: In my opinion it is altogether possible in our society to be a good Christian or a good Jew, that is, a loving human being, without starving to death. What matters is your level of competence and the courage needed to adhere to the truth and persist in love rather than give yourself up for the sake of your career.

But all that notwithstanding, it remains a fact that Christian or Jewish morality is incompatible with the morality of success, of ruthlessness, of selfishness, of not giving, of not sharing. Since that point will be obvious to anyone who reflects on it, I needn't dwell on it here. Anyway, this double standard in our morality has been described and criticized often. To sum up, then, the "ethic" that dominates in modern capitalism has amputated religion's other leg. Religion no longer functions as a promulgator of values, for people no longer trust it in that role either. God has abdicated both as the creator of the world and as the spokesman for values like love of neighbor and the overcoming of greed. But humanity does not seem either willing or able to do without religion entirely. Man does not live by bread alone. He has to have a vision, a faith, that awakens his interest and elevates him above mere animal existence. A regression to earlier heathenism and worship of idols holds no attraction for modern man, but I think we can say that our century is developing a new religion, one I would like to call the "religion of technology."

There are two particular aspects of this religion I would like to mention here. One is the promise of the Big Rock Candy Mountain, the dream of unlimited and instant gratification. New needs are being produced every minute; there is no end to them; and humankind, like an eternal suckling babe, waits with open mouth, expecting to be fed more and more and more. This is a paradise of total gratification, a paradise of superfluity that makes us lazy and passive. Technology's goal becomes the elimination of effort.

The other aspect of this religion is more complex. Ever since the Renaissance, humanity has concentrated its intellectual efforts on penetrating and understanding nature's secrets. But nature's secrets were, at least to some extent, also the secrets of nature's creator. For four hundred years man has invested his energies in plumbing nature's mysteries so that he will be able to control nature. His most deep-seated motive was to cease being a mere spectator of the natural world and to become able to create that world himself. It is difficult to express precisely what I want to say here, but if I were to state what I mean in its most radical form, I would have to say: Man wanted to become God himself. What God was able to do, man wanted to be able to do, too. I think the spectacle and the enthusiasm we witnessed when the astronauts first set foot on the moon had the quality of a pagan religious ceremony. That moment represented man's first step on the way to overcoming his human limitations and becoming God. Even Christian newspapers were saying that the conquest of the moon was the greatest thing to happen since the creation of the universe. Now it is a bit imprudent of Christians to say that—after the creation itself—there is another event more important than the Incarnation. But that was all forgotten in the moment when people were themselves witness to the fact of man's stepping outside the laws that had limited him before, overcoming the force of gravity, and setting out on a path into infinity.

Now you may feel that I'm exaggerating a bit here, but what I want to do is call your attention to tendencies that are still hidden below the surface. Was the hysterically enthusiastic response to the landing on the moon no more than applause for a scientific success? Hardly. There have been far more fantastic scientific achievements that have stirred up not the slightest public interest. What we have here is something altogether new. We are witnessing the emergence of a new form of idolatry. Technology is the new God, or man himself is becoming God, and the astronauts are the high priests of this religion. That is why they draw so much adulation. But no one admits this, because we are, after all, Christians or Jews, or at least not heathens. That is why we have to cover up what we are doing, rationalize it. But behind all the sleight-of-hand a new religion is, I think, taking shape, one in which technology is assuming the role of a Great Mother who will feed all her children and satisfy all their demands. The picture is not as simple as I am painting it here, because there are a number of complex, interlocking motives underlying the new religion. But we can safely say that the new religion has no moral principles to promulgate, except one, which is that we have to do whatever is technologically possible to do. Technological capability has become a moral obligation, has become the very source of our morality.

Dostoevski said that if God is dead then anything is permitted. He assumed that all previous morality had been based on belief in God. But if people no longer believe in God, if God is no longer a reality that forms their thoughts and actions, then we have good reason to ask whether they will not become totally immoral, whether they will not stop looking to any kind of moral principles for guidance. That is a question we have to take seriously, and if we are feeling pessimistic, we may conclude that it is exactly what has happened and that our morality is continuing to decline all the time. There are significant differences between now and earlier times. In 1914, for example, the warring nations adhered to two internationally accepted rules. Civilians were not killed, and no one was tortured. Today it is taken for granted that civilians will be killed in the course of any and all hostilities, because warring parties no longer accept any limitations on their use of force. Then, too, technology cannot make allowances for that kind of differentiation. Technology kills anonymously; we kill by pressing a button. Because we do not see our opponent, we are not moved to sympathy or compassion. And torture is the rule today, not the exception. Everyone tries to deny that, but it is a generally known fact. The use of torture to obtain information is widespread. We would be astonished to know in how many countries of the world torture is used.

Perhaps we needn't say that cruelty is on the increase, but it would be hard to deny that humanity and the moral prohibitions that go with it are declining. That has brought about a great change in the world, but on the other hand we can see that new moral principles are coming to the fore; we find them in the younger generation, for example, in their struggle for peace, for life, against destruction and war. They are not just mouthing empty phrases. Many young people (and not just young ones) are proclaiming their allegiance to other, better values and goals. Millions of people have become sensitive to the destruction of life on so many fronts, to inhumane wars in which there is not even a pretense of self-defense. We see a new morality of love taking shape, too, in opposition to the consumer society. The new morality may have its flaws, but it remains impressive in its protest against empty forms and words. We see evidence of a new morality, too, in the self-sacrifices made in the political realm, in the numerous struggles for liberation and self-determination that are going on today.

Those are encouraging developments, and because of them I feel that Dostoevski was wrong in linking moral principles so closely to a belief in God. Buddhism provides us with a glowing example of how some cultures develop moral principles without any authoritarian or patriarchal underpinnings. Those principles are rooted and flourish, if you will, in a humane soil. That is to say, human beings cannot live, they become confused and unhappy, if they do not acknowledge a principle that they and all those around them look to as a guiding principle for their lives. This principle cannot be forced on them; it has to emerge from them. I cannot go into the many aspects of this question now. All I mean to show, as I mentioned initially, is that people have a deeply rooted need to act morally. Immorality causes them to lose their inner harmony and balance. And it is immorality going under the guise of morality if people are told that they have to kill, that they have to obey, that they should pursue only their own selfish interests, that sympathy will be a hindrance to them, and so forth. If voices of that kind grow too loud they can drown out a person's own inner voice, the voice of his humanistic conscience. Then he may get the idea that if God is dead, anything and everything is permitted.

Expanding the Range of Human Growth

The younger generation is playing a central role in the moral crisis we are currently experiencing. I'm thinking in particular of the radicals among our young adults, and when I say "radicals" I don't mean the ones who call themselves radicals and seem to think they can justify any and all violence by calling it "radical." Many young people are simply childish, not radical. Lenin dealt with that subject in his essay on the childhood diseases of Communism.

But there are large numbers of young people who are radical not just in their political demands but in another respect that is closely linked to the subject of the last section, that is, to the rejection of authoritarian morality. The rebellion is directed not solely at authority (all revolutions voice a protest against authority) but at the patriarchal principle and the morality rooted in that principle, a morality that calls obedience a virtue and disobedience a sin. A phenomenon of great significance that follows from this morality is that people develop guilt feelings if they do not do what they are supposed to do. Instead of doing what their own hearts, their own feelings, their own humanity tells them to do, they submit to an authoritarian order that punishes them with guilt if they violate it.

What characterizes a large number of young people and what makes them so likable for so many of the rest of us, myself included, is, I think, that they have freed themselves from the guilt feelings imposed by authoritarian morality. They have, by and large, discarded the guilt that has been drilled into Western humankind in the Judeo-Christian tradition for the last two thousand years and put aside the fear of acting outside the norms that have determined our behavior to such a great extent. But in doing so they have not become immoral themselves. On the contrary, they are in search of new principles of morality.

And here I have to mention another distinctive feature of this young generation: a new honesty. They do not feel the same compulsion that earlier generations did to make up excuses for themselves, to rationalize, to refuse to call a spade a spade. One result is that they sometimes use language that is of questionable taste and that puts off people raised in the old tradition. But the key point is that they give expression to an honesty that is completely at odds with the dishonesty prevalent in bourgeois, patriarchal society, where we always have to hide what we feel guilty about and where we always have to act as if we were the very incarnation of all good qualities. We cannot admit that "nothing human is alien to us," because such an admission would push us to the brink of disobedience. But at the moment when we understand and acknowledge that the reality of man includes both his best and his worst, at that moment we become fully human. Instead of feeling outraged over our negative potential, we have to experience that, too, as part of our humanity.

Sigmund Freud contributed a great deal to the new honesty. Indeed, he opened up a wholly new dimension of honesty. Before Freud we took it at face value when people assured us of their "good intentions." But now, after Freud's discovery and systematic study of the unconscious, asseverations of good intentions won't do any more. We want to know what the unconscious motives behind those good intentions are. And we have come to the realization that it makes little difference whether someone is aware of his bad intentions or whether he is simply clever enough to rationalize them and so hide them both from others and himself. Indeed, someone with truly evil intentions may have achieved greater honesty with himself than someone who has repressed his evil intentions from his conscious mind and is therefore in an even better position to carry them out because he can package them in the guise of good and virtuous ideas.

Ever since Freud, we have had to face the fact that we are responsible not only for our conscious minds and our "good intentions" but also for our unconscious. Our actions and not our words alone speak for us. It's even possible that our words mean nothing at all. However, Freud's work is not the only reason we have for being suspicious of mere words. We have also had the experience of seeing human dishonesty lead us into wars in which hundreds of millions of people were killed or, for the sake of "honor," voluntarily marched off to their deaths. All those deaths can be traced back to lies and empty slogans. We have good reason today to be less impressed than ever by what people say. Words and ideas come cheap and can be done up in all kinds of packages. That's why young people are less inclined to ask, "What did you think about all that?" and ask instead, "What did you do? What were your motives?"

I think this effect of Freud's work, the introduction of a new honesty into our lives, is of far more importance in the development of the Western world than the "sexual revolution" whose beginnings are usually traced back to him. In a society that is as totally oriented to consumption as ours is, the sexual revolution, if that's what you want to call it, probably would have come about without Freud. We cannot exhort people to obtain everything they need to satisfy their senses and at the same time urge sexual abstinence on them. In a consumer society sex will inevitably become a consumer article. A number of industries depend on that fact, and a lot of money is spent to maintain the attractiveness of sexuality. That represents a change from earlier times but no revolution. And it would be difficult to lay that change at Freud's door.

What is both new and positive, however, is that for young people sexuality is no longer burdened with guilt feelings. I'd like to take a minute here to examine the link between sexuality and guilt feelings more closely. If authoritarian ethics declares sexual drives "sinful," the result for all of us is an inexhaustible source of guilt, and we could say that from our third year on every one of us has a massive bank account of guilt feelings saved up. Because human beings, constituted as they are, cannot help having sexual desires, they also cannot help feeling guilt if those feelings have a stigma attached to them. Restrictions placed on sexuality lead to guilt feelings that are then generally exploited to create and maintain an authoritarian ethic.

The younger generation (and the older one, too, to some extent) finally seems to have rid itself of that kind of guilt. That is no small advance. But if you'll forgive me for belaboring the obvious, I have to add here that all is not gold that glitters. Because of our consumer orientation, sex is exploited increasingly to disguise a lack of intimacy. We use physical closeness to gloss over the human alienation we feel. Physical intimacy alone cannot create emotional intimacy. Emotional intimacy, a genuine harmony between two people, may well be linked with physical intimacy, may even begin with it, and can be confirmed again and again by it, but those two kinds of intimacy are not identical. At those moments when we lack emotional intimacy we are most likely to substitute physical intimacy for it. And if we are normally constituted both physically and mentally, that is quite easy to do.

The younger generation, as I have said, rejects the patriarchal order and consumer society as well. But it is given to another kind of consumerism, which is exemplified in young people's use of drugs. Their parents buy cars, clothes, jewelry; the children take drugs. There are many reasons why they reach for drugs and tend to develop an ever greater dependency on them, reasons that demand our careful consideration; but whatever else drug dependency is, it is also an expression of that same lazy, passive *Homo consumens* that the children criticize in their parents but that they themselves also represent in a different guise. The young people, too, are always waiting for something to come to them from the outside, waiting for the high of drugs, the high of sex, the high of the rock rhythms that hypnotize them, carry them off, sweep them away. Those rhythms do not encourage activity. They transport the young into an orgiastic state, into a state like a drug high, in which they forget themselves and so are profoundly passive. An active human being does not forget himself; he is himself and is constantly becoming himself. He becomes more mature, he becomes more adult, he grows. A passive person is, as I suggested before, an eternal suckling babe. *What* he consumes is ultimately of little consequence to him. He simply waits with open mouth, as it were, for whatever the bottle offers. Then he is gradually sated without having to do anything himself. None of his psychic powers is called into play, and finally he grows tired and sleepy. The sleep he experiences is often a narcosis, an exhaustion induced by boredom, more than a sleep of healthy regeneration. Once again you may feel that I am exaggerating here, but estimates suggest that more people than we would imagine are having that kind of experience. And the media involved in producing our false needs keep reassuring us that it is our level of consumption that demonstrates the high level of our culture.

The question we have to ask in our society of bad, superfluous affluence that no one can possibly digest and that contributes nothing to our vitality—the question we have to ask is whether we can still manage, in principle at least, to create a good affluence. Can we somehow make good, truly productive use of the overabundant production we are technologically capable of, a use that serves human beings and their growth? That should be possible if we will understand that what we have to do is encourage and satisfy only *those* needs that make people more active, livelier, freer, so that they will not be driven by their feelings or simply react to stimuli but will be open and attentive and determined to realize their own potential, to enliven, enrich, and inspire themselves and others. One prerequisite for accomplishing that is, of course, to reorganize not only our work but also our so-called leisure. Our free time is, for the most part, nothing but lazy time. It provides us with an illusion of power because we can bring the world into our living rooms by pressing a button on the TV set or because we can get behind the wheel of a car and fool ourselves into thinking the engine's 100 horsepower is our own. We have truly "free time" only to the extent that we cultivate needs that are rooted in man and that move him to become active. That is why work has to stop being monotonous and boring. And the central problem we face in organizing our work is: How can we make work interesting, exciting, lively?

Here we come up against an even more basic question: What is the point of our work? Is it to increase production and consumption? Or is it to promote the development and growth of human beings? It is usually claimed that the one cannot be separated from the other. What is good for industry is good for people, and vice versa. That sounds like the proclamation of some lovely, preordained harmony, but in fact it is an outright lie. It is easy to demonstrate that many things that were beneficial to industry were bad for people. And that is our dilemma today. If we continue on the path we are on, progress will be achieved only at the expense of human beings. And so we have to make a choice. To put it in biblical language, we have to choose between God and Caesar. That may sound very dramatic, but if we are going to talk seriously about life, then things do get dramatic. What I have in mind here is not only the question of life and death but also whether we will choose the increasing death in the life we see around us or will opt for lives of vitality and activity. The whole point of life is to become increasingly vital, more full of life. People deceive themselves about that. They live as if they have stopped living or as if they have never begun to live.

Our folk wisdom tells us that everyone over forty is responsible for his own face. That means that our own life histories will reveal whether we have lived our lives rightly or wrongly (not rightly or wrongly in a moral sense but in terms of our own unique being). And the most glowing funeral orations with their lists of achievements cannot gloss over the crucial question that we must not avoid answering: Were we or are we truly alive? Do we live our own lives, or are they lived on someone else's terms? I agree with thinkers like Marx and Disraeli, who were convinced that luxury is no less an evil than poverty. And by luxury they meant what we have been calling superfluous affluence here. But if we want to make genuine abundance our goal instead, we will have to make some fundamental changes in our ways of living and thinking. I am, of course, fully aware of the great difficulties that lie in the way of effecting such changes.

I think that the changes can be effected only if people feel a deep need for more life and less routine, only if they reject boredom and respond to needs that make them more vital and spontaneous, freer and happier. Many nations (mainly the underdeveloped ones) dream that they would be happy if they only had everything the Americans have. But America is where more people than in any other country have learned that all our modern comforts do is tend to make us passive, impersonal, and manipulable rather than happy. It is no coincidence that our rebellious youth comes primarily from the middle and upper classes, in which superfluous affluence is most apparent. That kind of affluence may make for happiness in our imaginations, in our fantasies, but it does not make us happy in our heart of hearts.

It seems extremely important to me to grasp clearly a principle that is essential to formulating our strategies in the art of living. We will botch our lives if we pursue conflicting goals and do not realize that they are at odds with each other and are mutually exclusive. You may be familiar with another experiment Pavlov conducted with a dog. The dog had been trained to expect food when he saw a circle and not to expect any when he saw an ellipse. Then, step by step, Pavlov made the shape of the ellipse approach that of the circle, until the two shapes so nearly resembled each other that the dog could not tell them apart. In this conflict situation, the animal became ill and showed the classical symptoms of neurosis. He became anxious, confused, and insecure.

Human beings too will become psychically ill if they pursue conflicting goals. They lose their equilibrium, their self-confidence, their powers of discrimination. They no longer know what is good for them. The first thing we have to do, then, is to ask ourselves in all honesty what the conflicting goals are that we are pursuing. Why are they incompatible? What damage is the conflict between them causing in us? These questions cannot be answered by speeches and certainly not by propaganda, which does nothing but make fanatics of people. Every single one of us should try to call himself to account and think something along this line: "You will live only a short time. Who are you, and what is it you really want?" If we give ourselves up to the kind of affluence that is ultimately poverty, ultimately misery, we shall be squelching the richness that is ready to unfold and flourish within us; and on our decision for superfluity or abundance, for a good or a bad affluence, depends no more nor less than the future of humankind.

On the Origins of Aggression

It is hardly surprising that we are devoting more and more attention to the problem of aggression these days. We have experienced wars in the past; we are experiencing them in the present; and we fear the atomic war for which all the major powers of the world are arming themselves. At the same time people feel powerless to change this state of affairs. They see that their governments, which appear to have applied all their wisdom and brought all their goodwill to the issue, have not yet been able even to slow down or stabilize the arms race. So it is quite understandable that people are eager, on the one hand, to know where aggression really comes from but, on the other, are also receptive to theories that say aggression is part of human nature, not something that man creates himself or that his social institutions inevitably produce. That is the position Konrad Lorenz made popular in a book he published some years ago. In *On Aggression* Lorenz argues that aggression is constantly and spontaneously being created in the human brain, that it is a legacy from our animal ancestors, and that it increases more and more, assuming larger and larger proportions, if there is no release for it. If there is due cause, it will be expressed. But if the provocations are very weak or are missing altogether, then the accumulated aggression will eventually explode. People can't help behaving aggressively after a certain period, because they have gathered so much aggressive energy inside them that it has to be released. We might call this a "hydraulic" theory. The greater the pressure becomes, the greater the likelihood is that the water or steam will burst out of its container. Lorenz illustrates his theory with an entertaining story about his aunt in Vienna. Every six months that lady would hire a new maid. (This story took place in the old days when maids were not the rarity they are now.) When the maid first arrived, Lorenz's aunt was always utterly delighted and full of great expectations. But after a week or two her enthusiasm began to wane. Disenchantment soon gave way to criticism and dissatisfaction, and finally, after about six months, she was so furious with the maid that she fired her. Lorenz's aunt went through this cycle more or less regularly every six months, and what Lorenz means to show with the story is how aggression gradually builds up until, at a certain point, it has to vent itself.

Now that may be how things look from the outside, but if we understand a little more about people than Lorenz does—he understands a great deal about animals—then we know how inadequate his explanation is. A psychoanalyst—and not only a psychoanalyst but almost anyone with a little insight into human nature—will assume that the aunt is a narcissistic, exploitive woman who would like to buy not just eight hours of work a day when she hires a maid but love, loyalty, devotion, amiability, and fifteen hours of work a day. She greets every new maid with those same expectations and is no doubt quite nice and charming to her, because she assumes that at last she has found the right one. But once she takes a closer look she finds that the maid will not measure up to her expectations at all. She becomes more and more disappointed and angry and finally fires the maid, hoping that the next one will prove to be the right one. Since she probably has very little to do, the search for the perfect maid provides some drama in her life and gives her something to talk about. It is probably the main focus of her conversations with her friends. None of her behavior has anything to do with accumulated aggression; it is instead the product of a very specific character structure. And I'm sure that at least the older people among you know any number of individuals who—whether there happen to be maids any more or not—would behave similarly in that kind of situation.

The theory of innate aggression, which I cannot go into in detail here, bears a certain relationship to the old theory of the death wish. It was Freud's assumption from the 1920s on that there were two basic drives in all people, in all cells, in any living substance: a will to live and a will to die. And the will to die— or, more exactly, this wish for death—could express itself in one of two ways. If it was turned outward, it manifested itself as destructiveness; if turned inward, it was a self-destructive force that led to illness, suicide, or, if merged with sexual impulses, masochism. The death wish, the theory holds, is innate. It is not affected by circumstances; it is not called into being by external forces. Man has only two choices: Either he can turn his wish for death and destruction against himself, or he can turn it against others. And that leaves him faced with a tragic dilemma indeed.

But in fact the scientists who have concerned themselves with this problem have been able to turn up very little evidence over the years to support the theory. The generally accepted view among psychologists today is that aggression is conditioned by the social environment or that it is "channeled" by specific stimuli, by the culture—in short, by any number of factors. But, for the reasons I mentioned before, Lorenz's theory of aggression gained great popularity in the general public. It deluded us into thinking there was nothing we could do after all. It provided us with a good excuse: If all this aggression and the dangers that go with it are in fact innate in us, we can't hope to run counter to our very nature, can we?

There have always been two fundamentally different views of human nature. One has claimed that man is evil and destructive by nature. That is why war is inevitable, and that is why we have to have strict authorities over us. Human beings have to be kept under control. We have to protect them from their own aggressiveness. The other view says that man is basically good, that it is only adverse social conditions that make him bad. If we change those conditions, then we can reduce the evil, the aggressiveness in man, or possibly even rid ourselves of it altogether. Those views represent extremes that both miss the mark. People who propound the natural, innate aggressiveness of man are inclined to overlook those many historical epochs, those many cultures, and those many individuals that have displayed a minimum of aggressiveness. If aggression were innate, such examples would never exist. On the other side of the fence, the optimists who are against war and for peace and social justice have often been inclined to at least underestimate the significance and strength of human aggressiveness, if not to deny it altogether. The philosophers of the Enlightenment in France took that position, and their optimism cropped up again in the works of Karl Marx and in the beliefs of the early socialists.

I personally advocate a third view, which is, however, closer to the second than to the first. I begin with the assumption that man is much more destructive and much crueler than animals. Animals are not sadistic; animals are not enemies of life. But human history is a chronicle of unimaginable cruelty and destructiveness. That record gives us no reason to make light of the strength and intensity of human aggressiveness. But I also think that the roots of our aggressiveness do not go back to our animal nature, our instincts, and our past, but that human aggressiveness, to the extent that it is greater than that of animals, can be explained by the specific conditions of human existence. Aggressiveness, or destructiveness, is an evil; it is not just a "so-called" evil, as Lorenz would have us believe. *But it is human.* It is a potential present in man, present in all of us, and it will come to the fore if our development does not take better, more mature directions.

The human "extra" of aggression, that measure of aggression in man that exceeds animal aggression, is rooted in human character. I do not mean character here in a legal sense but in a psychoanalytical sense: character as a system of relationships that link an individual to the world. By character I mean what man has created to replace the animal instincts that are only minimally developed in him. What I am saying about character here may sound somewhat theoretical, but if you look back on your own experience I'm sure that many of you will understand precisely what I am driving at when I speak of character in that sense. You will surely have come across people whom you would identify as having a sadistic character. And you will also have met others whom you would characterize as "kindly." When you make those judgments you are not saying that this man once did something sadistic or that that one was once very friendly. You are referring instead to a quality of character that runs through the individual's entire life. There are sadistic individuals who never do anything sadistic because they never have the opportunity to, and only a very acute observer will ever catch them red-handed in some small sadistic act. Conversely, there are characters that are not basically destructive, yet individuals of this kind may shoot someone else down in a fit of rage or despair. But that does not by any means indicate that their characters are essentially destructive.

If we assume that evil is human, that is, rooted in man's specifically human condition and not in his animal past, then we can avoid a logical paradox that the theoreticians of instinct cannot escape, try as they might. They claim that man's greater aggressiveness can be explained from the lesser aggressiveness of animals. How can that be? We cannot assume that what man has inherited from the animals has made him much more aggressive and destructive than animals have ever been. The more logical conclusion is that human behavior that differs from animal behavior—in this case, man's greater cruelty—is not something man has inherited from animals but something originating in the specific conditions of human existence.

But now let me make a few remarks about *animal aggressiveness.* Animal aggressiveness is attuned to biological needs. It serves the survival of the individual and of the species, and it is mobilized whenever there is an external threat to the animal's vital interests, for example, whenever he is faced with a threat to his life, his food, his relations with animals of the opposite sex, his territory, or the like. If threatened, animals—and human beings—will react with either aggressiveness or flight. If no threat is present, no aggression will be mobilized. Aggressiveness is present in the brain as a mechanism that can be activated at any time but does not accumulate and does not have to be vented in actions if there is no particular stimulus or occasion for such behavior. It does not, in other words, reflect the "hydraulic" model. The neurophysiologist Hess was the first to make that very clear when he showed which centers or which areas of the brain produced aggressiveness when the appropriate stimuli were present and when a threat to vital interests mobilized those centers.

The aggressiveness of predators is a different matter. Predators do not attack only when they are threatened. They attack to obtain their food. That predatory aggressiveness is located, neurophysiologically, in centers of the brain different from the ones that control defensive aggression. On the whole, then, we find that animals are generally not very aggressive at all, unless they happen to be threatened. Blood is rarely spilled among animals, even when they actually fight. Observation of chimpanzees, sacred baboons, and other primates has shown how extraordinarily peaceful the social life of those primates actually is. We can probably safely say that if humanity displayed no more aggression than the chimpanzees, we wouldn't have to worry about war and aggression at all. The same is true of wolves. Wolves are predators, and if they attack a sheep, they are of course aggressive. Human beings imagine the wolf to be an incredibly aggressive creature. But in doing so they confuse his aggressiveness in finding food with his aggressiveness when he is not hunting for food. Wolves among themselves are not the least bit aggressive; they are downright friendly. It is therefore unjust to characterize human aggressiveness by comparing it with aggressiveness among wolves, as we do when we say that one man behaved toward another as one wolf did toward another (*homo homini lupus*). We could possibly say "as a wolf behaved toward a sheep" but not "as a wolf did toward a wolf."

We can see, then, that animal aggressiveness does not follow the hydraulic model. As long as the animal is not threatened, there is no constantly increasing aggressiveness that finally produces an explosion. To put it another way, human aggressiveness is a possibility provided by biology and present in the brain, but its activation is not a necessity. It will not manifest itself unless the need for self-preservation sets it in motion. That is an important difference from the behavioristic thesis holding that aggressiveness is a learned trait and that it is circumstances and circumstances only that make people aggressive. Things aren't that simple either, for if aggressiveness could be taught only by circumstances, it could not move into action as quickly and intensely as it does and as it in fact must. The reality is that aggressiveness is a biological given, a possibility that is present and that can be mobilized very quickly. All the neurophysiological mechanisms necessary for its activation are there and functional in us, but, as I have said, they have to be mobilized first, and without mobilization they do not go into action. Let me illustrate the point with a graphic example. If, for self-defense, someone keeps a revolver next to him on his bed at night or in his desk during the day, that does not mean he intends to shoot that revolver all the time. But it does mean that he will use it in case of danger. That is precisely the way the physiology of our brain is organized. There is a revolver present in our brain, as it were, always ready for quick action in case of an attack. But contrary to what the instinct theory claims, the existence of that state of preparedness does not result in a piling up of aggression that eventually has to explode.

Then, too, Hess and other neurophysiologists have found that animals respond to danger not only with attacks but also with flight. Attack is the last resort the animal takes when its chances of flight are cut off. Only then does it attack; only then does it fight.

And if we are to speak of an "aggressive instinct" in human beings, then we must also speak of a flight instinct as well. If the proponents of a theory of aggression and of instinct say man is constantly prodded on by aggressive feelings that he can control only with the greatest of difficulty, we are obliged to add that man is also motivated by an almost irresistible urge to flee, and this impulse, too, can be controlled only with the greatest of difficulty. Anyone who has ever observed combat knows very well how strong the human impulse to flee is. Otherwise we would not need the laws that often punish military desertion with death. In other words, the human brain provides us with two possibilities for reacting to an attack: We can fight or we can flee. But both the flight impulse and the attack impulse remain inactive if there is no threat, and they do not automatically produce a constantly active and ever increasing tendency for aggression or flight.

We have seen that the "hydraulic" theory of aggression as presented by Lorenz, and to some extent by Freud in his death wish theory, is not tenable. Neurophysiological findings show that neither human or animal aggressiveness is a constantly growing, spontaneously self-activating drive but is mobilized by stimuli carrying a threat to either the human being's or the animal's existence or vital interests. But there are reasons other than physiological ones that make the "hydraulic" theory untenable. It collapses, too, in the face of facts we can marshal from anthropology, paleontology, psychiatry, and social psychology. If the theory were correct, then we would expect that on the whole aggressiveness would be about the same in all individuals and in all cultures and societies. We would, of course, make allowance—as we do with intelligence—for differences in intensity, relatively small though those differences are. But by and large people everywhere should display the same amount of aggressiveness and destructiveness. But that is simply not the case.

Let's begin with the anthropological data. There are many primitive tribes in which no marked aggressiveness appears at all and in which, on the contrary, a spirit of friendliness predominates. In descriptions of such tribes we find a number of traits that commonly occur together and form a syndrome: minimal aggression (and, concomitantly, no crime and almost no murder), no private property, no exploitation, and no hierarchies. Tribes of that kind occur among the Pueblo Indians, but similar ones can be found all over the world. Colin Turnbull has given us a fascinating description of a tribe whose members are not farmers like the Pueblo Indians but are extremely primitive hunters not much different from the hunters of 30,000 years ago. It is a pygmy tribe that lives in the jungles of central Africa. Aggression is almost nonexistent among these people. Individuals do, of course, get angry occasionally, and then observers whose theories about aggression differ from mine will say: "There, you see? That man there is angry." But I must say I find that a rather petty way of looking at things, for it is one thing if a person gets angry now and then and quite another if he is so overloaded with aggression that it prompts him to want war, to kill people, and so on. There is a huge difference between a person who may get angry occasionally and one who is destructive and full of hate; anyone who fails to see that difference is, I feel, a rather obtuse observer.

The pygmy hunters regard the jungle in which they live as their mother; like all hunters, they kill only as many animals as they need to eat. Putting stores away for the future is out of the question, because they have no way to preserve their meat. When they need food, they hunt. There is no great surplus, but by and large they have enough to live on. That is why there is no private property. And they have no leader. Why, indeed, should they? Their lives are governed by the demands of their situation, and everyone knows what his task is. If we wanted to put it that way, we could say that these tribes possess a deeply rooted sense of democracy. No one tells anyone else what to do. There is no reason why anyone should. He could not gain any advantage by doing so. And, of course, there is no exploitation. Why would anyone want to make use of another's labor? Should I send someone out to do my hunting for me? That would make life awfully boring. And then what else is there to do? There's really nothing he can do for me. Family life is peaceful. Monogamy, with the possibility of easy divorce, is the rule. Sexual relations before marriage are permitted. Sexuality is not burdened with any guilt feelings. A couple will ordinarily marry when the woman becomes pregnant, and the partners remain together for life, unless they should develop a disliking for each other at some point. But that rarely happens.

The pygmies are carefree, too, even though the hunt does not always go smoothly. Sometimes there is a shortage of game; sometimes they have lean years. But they trust the jungle to nourish them. They are not possessed by the idea that they have to use more, save more, have more, and that is why they are generally quite content. Tribes like this are the truly affluent societies—not because they are so wealthy but because they do not want more than they have. And what they have is enough to provide them with a secure and enjoyable life.

I want to stress particularly how important it is to see the entire system and structure here and not just to isolate one feature from it. If you ask simply, "Is this aggressiveness or isn't it?" you'll have difficulty answering. But if you take in the whole social structure, then you will see that you are dealing here with basically friendly people who are not fighting among themselves or jealous of each other and whose lack of aggression is an element we would logically expect, given their overall psychic and social orientation. And you will see, too, how closely the psychic system is linked to the social one.

One of the most interesting epochs in human history is the so-called Neolithic revolution. That revolution accompanied the development of agriculture in Asia Minor about 10,000 years ago. It is very likely, although we have no proof as yet, that it was women who discovered agriculture, and what they discovered was that *wild* grasses could be raised and improved to yield edible wheat and other grains. The men were not so ingenious. In that same period they were probably still hunting or were acquiring and caring for flocks of sheep. With the discovery of agriculture came the awareness that one's food need not be limited only to what nature provided of its own accord, but one could also take a creative hand in the natural process. Using one's intelligence and skills, one could produce something. As I said, it happened only a short time ago. In the early years of this revolution—let us say in the first four thousand—you would no doubt have found remarkably peaceful societies, ones in many respects like those of the North American Pueblo Indians. They were probably even matriarchal in organization and inhabited small villages. They produced a little more than they needed at any given moment, and that surplus gave them added security and allowed their populations to grow. But they did not have so much surplus that one group would envy another and want to take away its surplus. Neolithic society, like the modern tribes I have just discussed here, was probably characterized by a genuinely democratic way of life and, as I said, by a much stronger role for women and mothers. Patriarchal organization came much later, about 4000 to 3000 B.C., a period in which everything changed. People were able to produce much more than they needed. Slavery was introduced. The division of labor became more pronounced. Armies were built up; governments were formed; wars were fought. Man discovered that he could use other men to work for him. Hierarchies formed, with kings at their heads. The kings were deputies of god and often filled the role of high priest. That situation encouraged the development of aggressiveness, for men now had the ability to rob, steal, and exploit. And natural democracy gave way to a hierarchy in which everyone had to obey.

At this point I'd like to say a few things about the causes of war. Proponents of the instinct theory often claim that war is caused by man's aggressive instincts. That is a very naive as well as a very incorrect view. First of all, we know that most wars come about because governments convince their populations that they are under attack, that they have to defend their most sacred values, their lives, their freedom, democracy, and Lord knows what else. The wave of enthusiasm for war lasts a few weeks and then is pretty much gone. Now people have to be threatened and punished to continue fighting. But if people were by nature so aggressive that war actually satisfied their aggressive instincts, then governments wouldn't have to take those measures. On the contrary, they would have to propagandize for peace all the time so that people wouldn't be constantly yearning for a war in which they could vent their aggression. But as we all know, that is not the way things are, and we can even identify quite precisely the period when war as an institution had its beginnings or, if you will, was invented. It was the period after the Neolithic revolution, the period that saw the rise of city-states, of kings, of armies, and of the capability to make war, take slaves, steal treasure, and so forth. There was no organized war among the hunter-gatherers and the primitive agricultural peoples, because the capability for it simply didn't exist.

What this discussion shows us is that a number of primitive

tribes have social systems in which friendliness and cooperation are predominant and aggression at a minimum. If that picture of primitive societies is correct, the "hydraulic" theory that identifies aggression as an instinct cannot be maintained. Another point we can cite against the instinct theory is that levels of aggression within a society can vary greatly. If we look at the early 1930s in Germany, for example, we find that the Nazis drew most of their support from the old petit-bourgeoisie and from officers and students whose careers had been crippled by postwar conditions. The Nazis found no emotional echo in the middle class and upper middle class. I don't mean to say that those classes did not acquiesce in the Nazi system, but the ardent Nazis did not come from those classes, much less from the working class. Convinced Nazis were, as we all know, more the exception than the rule in the working class, though, oddly enough, convinced anti-Nazis were also an exception among workers. Why that is so is another question altogether.

We find a similar situation in the American South. The poor whites in the South have an incredible store of aggressiveness, much more than the Southern middle class and more too than the working class either in the South or on the American East Coast. Aggressiveness is always most present in those classes that are on the lowest social level, at the bottom of the social pyramid. Those are people who have few pleasures in life, who are uneducated, who see themselves being slowly squeezed out of the social mainstream, who are lacking in motivation and interests. Such people build up vast amounts of sadistic rage that does not develop in people who are productively occupied and who feel fully engaged in—or at least not totally excluded from—the social process. Those latter people have interests; they have the feeling that they are in step with the rest of society. That is why those classes do not develop the same measure of sadism and aggression that the old petit-bourgeoisie in Germany did or that certain classes in America do.

Levels of aggressiveness will differ in individuals, too. Take the patient who comes to a psychiatrist and says, "Doctor, I hate everybody. I hate my wife. I hate my children. I hate the people I work with. There's nobody I don't hate." For the psychiatrist, and I would hope for almost anyone else, too, that patient has rendered his own diagnosis and declared himself sick. We don't respond to such a person by saying, "But of course, everything is perfectly clear. We have here a case of the aggressive instinct at work." We say instead that this man's character is so constituted that it constantly produces aggression. We then ask: How did this person get this way? We inquire into the social circumstances of his life, his family history, his past experiences. We try to understand why such a high level of aggressiveness became part of this individual, part of his character structure. We do not say, as the advocates of the instinct theory say when they talk about war: "There's nothing you can do about it. This case just proves all over again how strong our inborn aggressiveness is."

All of us know aggressive people, and by aggressive I don't mean just quick-tempered. I mean destructive, hostile, sadistic people. And we all know friendly people who strike us as being warm and nonaggressive not just on a superficial level but at their very core. Their friendliness cannot in any way be equated with weakness or servility. If we are unaware of such differences, then we are in a bad way—and many people are in a bad way, because they do not notice those differences. But most people who take the trouble to look around them with any care know very well that those characterological differences exist.

Now we have to take a closer look at what we mean by specifically *human aggression.* Up to this point, all we have done is demonstrate that it does not function on the hydraulic model. We can distinguish between two basic types of aggressiveness in human beings. The first is, if you will, the biologically programmed type, the same defensive mechanism that we find in animals. The second is a specifically human kind of aggression that we do not find in animals. The latter type takes the form of human cruelty on the one hand and, on the other, of that passionate enmity toward life, that hatred of life that we call necrophilia, a subject I cannot go into in detail here.

Let's begin with the first type, that is, the biologically programmed human aggressiveness, which is identical to animal aggression. As we have seen, the animal's neurophysiological organization, which is the same in man, makes it react aggressively if its vital interests are threatened. A human being responds the same way. But in humans the reaction, this *reactive or defensive aggressiveness,* is much more extensive. There are three reasons. One is that the animal experiences only present threats. All it knows is: "At this moment I am threatened." The human being, with his mental powers, can imagine the future. Consequently, he can experience a threat that may not exist now but may well exist in the future. He therefore reacts aggressively not only to threats existing at the moment but also to ones in the future. That provides the reactive aggression with a much larger field in which to function, for the number of human beings is very large, as is the number of situations in which a threat to them may exist in the future.

Another reason why reactive aggression has a larger playground in humans is that humans are subject to suggestion while animals are not. You can convince a human being that his life or his freedom is threatened. You use words and symbols to do that. An animal cannot have its "brain washed," because it lacks the symbols, the words, essential to brainwashing. If you convince a man that he is threatened, his subjective reaction will be the same as if he actually were threatened. It makes no difference to his reactions that he only believes himself threatened. I do not have to speak at any length about the many cases in which wars were made possible because people had been made to believe they were threatened. The power of suggestion had created the aggressiveness needed to drive men into battle.

Then there is still a third and final reason. A human being has special interests that are closely linked to the values, ideals, and institutions with which he identifies. An attack on the ideals or persons central to his life, on the institutions that are sacred to him, can be as threatening to him as an attack on his life or on his source of food. Any number of things can be so precious to him: the idea of freedom, the idea of honor, his parents, his father, his mother, in some cultures his ancestors, the state, the flag, the government, religion, God. Any of those values, institutions, or ideals may be as important to him as his own physical existence. If they are threatened, he reacts with hostility.

If we put all three factors together, we can understand why defensive hostility in man is so much more extensive than it is in animals, even though the mechanism in which it is based is identical in man and animal. Man experiences many more threats, or experiences more things as threats, than the animal possibly can.

Man and animal share the biologically programmed, reactive aggressiveness that serves the defense of their vital interests. In man, however, there are kinds of aggressiveness that are not biologically given and do not serve the end of self-defense but are rooted in his character. The reasons why an individual develops that kind

51

of aggressive character are complicated, and I cannot go into them here. But aggressive characters of this sort are a reality and one that occurs only among human beings. What I want to focus on next is the phenomenon itself, the sadistic character as such.

When we speak of *sadism* we often have only the sexual perversion in mind, cases in which, say, a man experiences sexual arousal only if he can beat or abuse a woman in some way. Sadism can also mean the passion or wish to do bodily harm to another person. The essence of sadism is, however, wanting to have *control* over another living being, complete and absolute control. The other creature can be an animal, a child, or another adult, but in every case the sadistic individual makes the other living creature his property, a thing, an object of domination.

If someone can make another person defenseless and force him to bear pain, that is an extreme form of control, but it is not the only one. That form of sadism occurs sometimes in teachers, sometimes in prison guards, and so on. It is clear that this kind of sadism, though not sexual in a narrow sense of the word, is nonetheless what we might call a heated, sensual form of sadism. But it is not the only form. Far more common is a "cold sadism" that is not at all sensual and has nothing whatever to do with sexuality but still displays the same essential quality that sensual and sexual sadism do: Its goal is domination, complete control over another person, being able to mold and shape him as the potter does his clay.

There are even benign forms of sadism with which you are all familiar. Such sadism can turn up in all sorts of people, but mothers and bosses are particularly prone to it. One person controls another not to his harm or disadvantage but to his advantage. He tells him what he should do. Everything the subordinate should do is spelled out for him, and it is all good for him. It may indeed be good for him—or perhaps we should say profitable—but the problem with it is that he loses his freedom and autonomy. The relationship of mothers to their sons or fathers to their sons are often colored by that kind of sadism, and the sadistic individual is, of course, totally unaware of any sadistic intent, because he "means so well." Even the victim of such sadism is unaware of it, because all he sees is how he is profiting from his situation. The one thing he does not see is that his soul is being damaged, that he is becoming a submissive, dependent, unfree human being.

Now I'd like to give you an example of an extreme form of

sadism, a man possessed by a passion for absolute omnipotence, a man who wanted to be God. We find just such a portrait in Camus's play *Caligula*. Caligula, the Roman emperor, was a tyrant with unlimited power. He may not have been so different from other people at first, but then he found himself in a situation where he felt he was not subject to the normal conditions of human existence, for there were no limits put on his power. The first thing he does is to seduce his friends' wives. His friends don't just find this out—he himself lets them know it in no uncertain terms. But they have to flatter him and pay him homage. Unless they want to be murdered, they mustn't ever let their anger or indignation show. Otherwise he will kill them, first one, then another, whenever the mood strikes him. He will kill them not because he can't stand them any more but because being able to kill whomever he wants is a sign of his power, his omnipotence. But even that power does not satisfy his longing for omnipotence, for the ability to kill is ultimately limited, too. As a result, his desire for omnipotence takes the form of what we might call a symbolic wish, one that Camus presents very skilfully in the play. Caligula wants the moon. If he were to say that today, we might find the expression rather odd. But a few decades ago the expression meant something like: "I want the impossible. I want the kind of power than no human being can have. I am the only person who matters. I am God. I have power over everyone and everything. What I want I can have."

A man with a passion for absolute control will try to circumvent, to overstep the limits inherent in human existence, for it is part of the human condition that we are not omnipotent. And if a man should gain much too much power, death will show him how powerless he is in the face of nature. Camus shows us very convincingly how Caligula is really not so different from other people until he becomes mad. Because he attempts to overstep the boundaries of human existence he goes mad, as anyone will who makes such an attempt and cannot find his way back to human territory. We see from this example that madness is not really a disease in the sense that we normally think of disease but a certain way of solving the problem of human existence. The madman denies the powerlessness inherent in us that torments us because, in his fantasies, he does not recognize any limits. He behaves as if no limits existed. But because powerlessness is a reality he will necessarily lose his mind if he insists on pursuing his goal. If we wanted to put it this way, we could speak not of an illness but of a philosophy or—to be more precise still—a form of religion. Madness is an attempt to negate and deny human powerlessness by pretending to oneself, with the aid of some very specific tactic, that one is not ultimately powerless.

Fifty years ago we may still have believed that Caligulas existed only in Roman history. The twentieth century since then has presented us with a whole new crop of Caligulas—in Europe, in America, in Africa, everywhere. And all those Caligulas are cut after the same pattern. They get a taste of unlimited power, and they then remain irrevocably and passionately committed to solving their existential problems by denying any limitations on their power. We can see that very clearly both in Stalin and in Hitler. The limitations of human existence are denied, and that opens the way for a certain kind of madness.

Fortunately, most people with the sadistic longing for complete control over others have to be satisfied with indulging their cold sadism in more modest forms, though obviously in forms that still provide them with satisfaction. We know that parents can behave sadistically toward their children, trying to exert absolute control over them. That is not as common today as it used to be, because children are not as ready to put up with it any more. But it was quite common twenty, thirty, and forty years ago. Doctors see many cases of children brought to hospitals with serious injuries resulting from parental blows and abuse. The number of cases of sadistic child abuse that come to light is only a very small percentage of the cases that actually occur. For both by law and by custom parents can do just about anything they want with their children as long as they can claim that it was done for the child's good and as long as the evidence of physical abuse is not too horrendous. One could write volumes about the degree of control parents exercise over their children and the amount of downright sadistic abuse they deal out to them. The same can be said of policemen, nurses, prison guards, and so on. Their power is not as great as Caligula's. They too have to obey orders; they are very small cogs in the machine; and they have very little say in things. But compared to the children, the patients, or the prisoners they deal with, their power is relatively great. And so you find a large number of sadists in those callings. I do not mean to say by this that most teachers or nurses are sadists. On the contrary, great numbers of people become teachers or nurses because they feel a deep need to help others, because they are favorably disposed toward others and love their fellow humans. I do not have those people in mind here but rather the ones who are acting out of just the opposite motives and are usually not aware that behind the rationalizations they construct for themselves a passion to control others is at work in them.

That same passion is very prevalent among bureaucrats, too. Let me give you an example that you have no doubt often encountered yourselves. Imagine a man behind the window in a post office. Fifteen people are waiting in line, and at closing time there are still two left. At the very stroke of five o'clock the man shuts his window, turning away those last two people who have been waiting half an hour. There is just the trace of a smile on the man's thin lips, a barely visible, sadistic smile. He is glad that those two people have to leave, that he has the power to make them wait in vain and have to return tomorrow. He could just as easily have taken another minute or two for them, but he does not. A kindly person would take the time, and that is what most people in that situation would do. The sadist closes his window not just because business hours are over but because it gives him pleasure to close it. And though he may not earn a very large salary, that sadistic pleasure is as good as money, and he wouldn't think of doing without it.

Now I'd like to cite the example of a sadist who did much worse things than just control others: Heinrich Himmler. I'm going to read you a short letter that he wrote to a high-ranking SS officer, Count Adalbert Kottulinsky. "Dear Kottulinsky, You have been very ill with a serious heart ailment. In the interests of your health, I am hereby ordering you to stop smoking completely for the next two years. After these two years are up you may submit to me a physician's report on the state of your health. On the basis of that report I will decide whether you may resume smoking or not. Heil Hitler!" That is not only exerting control over another person but humiliating him as well. Himmler treats this adult like a stupid schoolboy. He writes in a way deliberately designed to humiliate. Himmler assumes control over Kottulinsky. He doesn't even let the doctor do the controlling and make the decision on whether Kottulinsky may or may not smoke again. Himmler arrogates this decision to himself.

Another trait of the bureaucrat as sadist is that he treats people like things. They become objects. He does not relate to them as human beings. Another characteristic is that only helpless individuals waken his sadistic interest, not ones who can defend themselves. A sadist up against a superior is usually cowardly, but someone who is helpless or can be made helpless—a child, a sick person, or, in certain political circumstances, a political opponent—those are the people who incite the sadist. He does not feel pity, as any normal person does, nor does he share the normal person's revulsion at the very idea of hitting someone who is defenseless. On the contrary, helplessness is the quality that stimulates the sadist, because it puts the possibility of absolute control within his reach.

Another trait of the sadist in bureaucrat's clothes is an excessive preoccupation with order. Order is everything. Order is the only sure thing in life, the only thing over which we can exert complete control. People with an excessive need for order are usually people who are afraid of life, because life is not orderly. It brings surprises; spontaneity is crucial to it. The only thing we can be sure of is death, but what life brings is always something new. The sadistic individual, though, who cannot relate to others and who sees everyone and everything in life as mere objects, that kind of person hates anything living, because it poses a threat to him. But he loves order.

It was therefore characteristic for Himmler to keep a diary—for ten years starting with his fourteenth year—filled with the most banal of entries. He notes how many rolls he ate, whether his train arrived on time or not. Every last little thing he did had to be recorded. Even as a young man he kept records of his correspondence in which he noted every letter he wrote or received. That is order. And we should add that it is the orderliness of a certain type, the orderliness of the old-fashioned bureaucrat for whom life means nothing but order and rules mean everything.

It is interesting to note in this context that when Eichmann was asked in Jerusalem whether he felt any guilt—he was interrogated by a very humane psychiatrist, and he apparently felt he could speak quite freely—he said yes, he did have some guilt feelings. And when asked what it was he felt guilty about, he replied: For having played hooky from school twice when he was a boy. That was not very clever of him as a defendant in the situation he was in. If he had wanted to be clever he could have said he felt guilty because he had murdered so many Jews. But he was perfectly honest, and it was quite natural for him to think of an incident when he had broken the rules. For the bureaucrat, there is only one sin, and that is to ‚violate the established order, to break the established rules.

A final trait of the sadistic character I want to mention is servility. The sadist wants to control the weak, but there is too little vitality in him to be able to live without submitting to someone stronger than himself. Himmler, for example, idolized Hitler. If the sadist does not subordinate himself to another person, then he may choose history, the past, the powers of nature, whatever it is that is stronger than he is. But the rule that always holds true is: I must submit, I must subordinate myself to a higher power, whatever that power may be. But those who are weaker than I am I will dominate. That is the system the bureaucratic sadist and the cold sadist in general live by.

The type I have been describing here is tellingly reflected in a characterization of Himmler that Carl J. Burckhardt wrote when he was a League of Nations commissioner in Danzig. "He creates an eerie impression with his quintessential subordination, his narrow-minded conscientiousness, his inhuman methodicalness, and the automaton-like quality of his behavior." That is a description par excellence of a cold sadist. Now you might ask: Mightn't Himmler have turned out quite differently if he had not been put in this situation, if there had never been such a thing as National Socialism? We can make an educated guess and say that he probably would have become a model civil servant. And I have no trouble at all imagining that at his funeral his immediate superior and his minister would have said of him: "He was a good father who loved his children and devoted all his energies to his work and to the organization he served." And that is indeed the kind of man Himmler was. We have to realize that even a sadistic man has somewhere in him the need to prove to himself that he is a human being, that he is capable of friendliness. If a person cannot demonstrate to himself that in some dimension of his being he is human, then he is on the verge of madness, for what he experiences at that point is an isolation from the rest of humankind that hardly anyone can bear. And it is a fact substantiated by the reports we have that many members of the units that carried out the execution of political prisoners, Jews, Russians, and others went mad, committed suicide, or suffered from a number of psychic disorders. A commander of one of those units even wrote that the troops had to be shown that the methods used to destroy the Jews, that is, shooting and gassing, were humane and militarily correct. Otherwise, the men's psychic equilibrium would be disturbed.

I think it is correct to say that there are many Himmlers, many sadists, who do not become openly sadistic simply because they are not given the opportunity to do so. But by the same token I think it would be false to say that there is a Himmler inside every one of us, that we all have sadistic tendencies that will come to the fore given the right circumstances. That is the very point I want to drive home here. There are sadistic character structures and nonsadistic ones. Some people, the ones with sadistic characters, will become openly sadistic if conditions allow them to. Others will not become sadists, no matter what the circumstances, simply because they have a different character. It is therefore important to understand this point and to learn to detect which people are sadistic and which are not. We cannot let ourselves be deceived by the fact that a person is very fond of children and animals and has done this or that good deed. Only if we perceive a person's character can we see what truly lies behind his consciousness, what it really is that motivates his overall behavior. We need to know which are the basic elements of his character and which are the more superficial, compensatory ones. I think it would be a great gain for us all if we understood more about character and were not so easily influenced by a person's outward behavior. It would be a great gain for us not only in our personal lives but also in our political ones. We might be able to forestall many a catastrophe if we could tell in advance whether the people who are so eager to guide our political fates are sadists or not.

Dreams Are the Universal Language of Man

W e all feel that we are fully at home only in one language, and we call that one our mother tongue. We may have learned a few foreign languages as well: French, Russian, Italian. But we forget that we all speak one other language, and that is the language of dreams. This language is a remarkable one. It is a *universal language* that has existed in all periods of human history and in all cultures. The dream language of primitive man, the dream language of Pharaoh in the Bible, the dream language of someone in Stuttgart or New York—they are all almost the same. We speak this language every night. Although we usually forget what we have dreamed and therefore think we haven't dreamed at all, we do dream ever single night.

What are the characteristics of dream language? Its most obvious characteristic, of course, is that it is a night language, a language of sleep. It's as if we could speak French only at night and didn't understand a word of it during the day. Furthermore, dream language is a symbolic language. We could say that the language makes use of visible, almost palpable things to express inner experiences in concrete form. That is just what literature does. If a writer says: "The red rose warms my heart," no one understands that to mean that the temperature has risen. The writer is referring to a feeling, an experience, that he expresses in the form of a concrete physical process.

Perhaps I can use the example of a very interesting dream to show what I mean here. Sigmund Freud had this dream and then related it afterward. It is his dream about a herbarium, and it is very short. Freud dreamed that he had a herbarium and that the herbarium had a dried flower in it. That is the whole dream. Freud had some ideas on what it meant. The flower was his wife's favorite flower, and his wife often complained that he never gave her flowers. Then, too, the flower was in some way linked to cocaine, of which he had become aware at just about the same time that its medical uses were being discovered. The flower in the herbarium was a simple symbol, but it was rich in meaning. It revealed something about one of the most important aspects of Freud's personality. Flowers are symbols of love, of sexuality, of the erotic, the living. But this flower in the herbarium is a dried one whose only remaining value is as an object of scientific scrutiny. It can be studied as an object of research but not experienced as something blossoming, living. If we look at Freud's attitude toward love and sexuality, we in fact find that although he made sex an object of scientific study, he was in his own life a rather shy and prudish man. When he was in his early forties, he wrote to a friend once that he was surprised at how attractive he found a woman he had seen. That is just one example of Freud's attitude toward life at an age when most men would not be the least surprised over such an occurrence. Thus, in this little symbol of a dried flower, a symbol that can be sketched in just a few words, we find clues to Freud's character that would oblige us to fill many pages if we were to attempt to spell out in detail everything that was implicit in the symbolic language of that brief dream.

Another important quality of dream language is that we know more about other people and ourselves when we are dreaming than we do when we're awake. We may be more irrational in our dreams—and I'll be coming back to this point later—but in a certain sense we are much wiser, much more perceptive. The example of Freud's dream shows this, too. As we know from Freud's own analysis of his dream, he was hardly aware of the aspect of his character that the dream reveals. But in this dream he could clearly recognize his equivocal attitude toward what the dream symbolized.

Related to this aspect of dream language is still another feature that most discussions of dreaming do not adequately acknowledge. Most people (I say "most people," but we have no stastics on this, so perhaps I should be more cautious and just say "many people" or, better still, "most of the people I have seen in my practice as a psychoanalyst") are creative in their dreams to an extent they never would have thought possible in their waking lives. In their dreams people who, when awake, would never manage to do anything of the sort, not even with the greatest of effort, become creators of stories, poems, myths. I don't know how many dreams I have heard that could be published word for word and that would give many a short story by Kafka a run for its money. And yet when that same individual is awake he would look at you as if you were mad if you were to say to him, "Well, now, write me a short story in Kafka's style." In fact he would be unable to write such a story. But in his dreams he is a poet, an artist, this same person who has no artistic capabilities at all when he is awake. To state my point in extreme form, we could say that a creative artist is someone who is creative without having to be asleep. In other words, he remains creative even though he is awake.

During the day we live in the context of a given culture. What we say in the daytime depends to a large extent on where we were born. It is obvious that an African who is a member of a hunting tribe will speak about other things and make use of other terms than we do. What we say is partially determined by our society. But in our dreams we speak a universal language. Our daytime language, whether our mother tongue or a foreign one, is always a socially determined language. Dream language, however, is a *universal language,* the *language of all mankind.*

What is the explanation for this capability? Let me begin with something that may seem complex but is actually quite simple: the difference between waking and sleeping. We spend our lives in two modes of existence that we take so much for granted that we are often not even conscious of them. We spend part of our time awake and part of it asleep. What does it mean, though, to say we are awake? When we are awake we are in a state that requires us to tend to our lives. We have to work; we have to acquire the things we need to live; we have to defend ourselves against attacks; in short, we are absorbed in the struggle for existence. And that struggle influences what we do and what we think. It influences what we do because we have to conform. We have to behave the way society expects us to behave so that we can produce, so that we can work. But more important still, this struggle strongly influences our feelings and the categories in which we think.

During the day we look at things the way we have to look at them to manipulate them, use them, make something out of them. We have to behave reasonably, and "reasonably" means the way other people do, so that they will understand us but also will like us and not think: That is a totally eccentric or insane person. We think and feel what "common sense" and so-called ordinary human decency tell us we should think and feel. We all think and feel that we love our parents, that they and all other authorities not only want the best for us but also know and do what is best, and so on. We feel happy or cheerful when the occasion demands, or if the occasion demands the opposite, we feel sad. In reality, we may not feel anything at all, but we think we do simply because we have assumed an appropriately happy or sad expression. And we do not think what strikes us as absurd because we assume that things that ought not to exist do not exist. Andersen's fairy tale about the emperor's new clothes illustrates that principle beautifully. The emperor is naked, but all the adults think he has gorgeous clothes on because that is what they expect. Only the little boy, whose thinking has not yet been pressed into the mold of most adults' daytime minds, can see that the emperor isn't wearing any clothes at all. When we are awake, we do, feel, and think what others expect of us.

Let me cite another dream that illustrates the same point. A high-ranking executive who is subordinate to only a single director in his firm had this dream. In his waking life, the executive has convinced himself that he is on very good terms with his boss. He likes him; he has no problems with him. Then he had this dream: His hands are tied together with a telephone cord, from which the phone is still dangling. Then he sees his boss, who seems to be asleep, lying next to him on the ground. The executive feels an overpowering rage. He finds a hammer, picks it up in both hands, and tries to smash the director's head with it. He hits the mark, but nothing happens. Then the director opens his eyes and smiles ironically at his attacker.

Though the man may have felt that he was on good terms with his boss, his dream tells us that he really hated his superior. He felt that the director oppressed him and kept him tied up.

He felt powerless and at his chief's mercy. That is the reality this man experienced in his dream. In his waking life that reality was, it seems, hidden from him.

What does the sleeping state give us that being awake cannot? We are free. That may sound like a strange thing to say, but in a certain sense we are free only when we are asleep. That is, when we are asleep we are no longer obliged to participate in the struggle for life. We do not have to conquer; we do not have to defend ourselves; we do not have to conform. We think and feel what *we* think and feel. Our thoughts and feelings in sleep are as subjective as they can get. In sleep, we don't have to *do* anything; we can simply *be.* In sleep we have no goals. We can experience the world as it really seems to us, as we really see it, and not the way it is *supposed* to look if we mean to achieve a certain goal. To put it another way, we can say that in sleep the unconscious has center stage. There is nothing at all mysterious about the unconscious. It means simply that in sleep we have access to what we don't know when we're awake. Or to put it the other way around: In the waking state we do not have access to what we know when we're asleep. We might even say that in the waking state the consciousness of sleep is unconscious, while in sleep the consciousness of waking is unconscious. There are two different types of consciousness involved. The one is operative in waking; the other, in sleeping.

Does that mean that we are more irrational in sleep, more subject to our drives? Yes, sometimes, but by no means always and not even in the majority of cases, even though Freud thought that dreams always pitted the irrational against the rational. But as I mentioned before, we often achieve greater insight and greater wisdom in our dreams because we are more independent, because we can see and feel without blinders on. Even in sleep we censor our dreams. We don't dare accept the freedom dream gives us, so we change and hide the real message of the dream the way we would if we wanted to prevent someone else from understanding what we really meant. In a case like that we are expressing, even in sleep, a reluctance to understand ourselves. That's why we often forget dreams, for most of them would not fit neatly into our waking lives. They would only disturb and irritate us.

In our dreams our creativity increases. We develop creative capabilities that we do not recognize, indeed, that we have no inkling of, when we are awake. I have in mind here a dream that another successful business executive had. (The dreams I am citing here do not come from patients of mine but from studies made of executive personalities.) This man felt very happy because he was successful. Judging by his income and the power he wielded, he had every right to feel that way, for we usually feel what we are expected to feel. So this man thought he was very happy. Then he had a dream. In the first part of the dream he is at a small lake. The lake is dirty. The atmosphere is dark, gloomy, grim. He recalls later, after the dream, that this lake is just like the one near which his parents had lived. The unpleasant memory is not just of the lake but also of the dreary, poverty-stricken mood of his childhood home. In the second scene of the dream he is in an extremely expensive car, driving up a mountainside on an ultramodern highway. He is driving fast; he has a feeling of power and success; and he is happy. Then comes a third scene, which takes place after he has reached the top of the mountain. Suddenly he is in a pornography shop. His wife was with him in the car, but now he is alone. No one else is there. Everything is dusty and dirty, and he feels totally alone and abandoned.

This dream tells us what the man really feels about his life and fate. Put in the simplest terms, the dream translates into something like this: When I was a child, everything around me was dismal and dirty. Now I'm a successful man who has driven to the peak of success with incredible speed. But ultimately, when this whole success game is over, I'll be right back in that same filth, that same poverty, that same sadness, that same isolation I experienced as a child. Everything will drop away, and I'll be right back where I started. The dream does not express a wish. It provides instead, in a creative, artistic language, a profound insight into the emptiness of the man's life.

We might say that many people are capable of that kind of creativity, but in the daytime they are so subject to the pressures of society—what Heidegger has called the "they"—that they lack the courage to be themselves and create something themselves. That is a sad commentary indeed on our society, which does not permit people to realize the creative capacities they have in them.

In our dreams we are telling ourselves something. As the Talmud (Berachot 55a) puts it: "A dream left uninterpreted is like a letter left unread." The word "interpret" is not really correct in this context. We do not have to interpret dreams. There is nothing to interpret. We do not have to interpret Chinese or Italian if we have learned those languages. Dream language is a language that we can learn, that has its own grammar, its own forms, a language that does not describe "facts" but conveys experience. It is easy to learn dream language, and you don't have to become a psychoanalyst to learn it. We could be learning it in school at the same time that we learn foreign languages. I feel it would be of great advantage for us to start learning dream language, because if we understand our dreams we will understand more about ourselves and others. I've said this could be an advantage to us, but it could also have its disadvantages. As a rule, we really don't want to know too much about ourselves or others. That knowledge can bother us. But the more we know about ourselves and the fewer illusions we have about others, the richer, stronger, more vital our lives will be. Then, too, if we understand dream language, we are not limited to the one-sided, intellectual perspective that has come to dominate most people's thinking in our time more than ever before in the past. We are not restricted to thinking *exclusively* in concepts but develop an eye for emotional differentiation. We integrate intellect and emotion and put unrealistic alternatives behind us. I am in no way propounding a dangerous anti-intellectualism here, much less a new sentimentality. But I do want to suggest that the language of dreams can teach us something that is essential to our lives, now more than ever: In our dreams we can become poets.

Psychology for Nonpsychologists

Premodern and Modern Psychology

Who is and who is not a psychologist? And what is psychology? The answer to the first question would appear to be quite simple. Anyone who has not studied psychology and has not earned an academic degree in that field is not a psychologist. That would mean practically everyone is a nonpsychologist. But that is not really the case, and I would go so far as to claim that there is no such thing as a nonpsychologist, because we all practice and have to practice our own brand of psychology as we live our lives. We have to know what is going on inside other people. We have to try to understand them. We even have to try to predict how others will behave. To do so we do not have to go to a university laboratory. The laboratory of everyday life (to which it is not even necessary to go) gives us ample opportunity to think through and ponder any number of experiments and cases. So we have asked the wrong question. We should ask not whether we are psychologists or nonpsychologists but whether we are good or bad psychologists. Whatever the answer to that question may be, I feel that the study of psychology can help us become better psychologists.

66

That brings us to our second question: What is psychology? This question is much harder to answer than the first one. We'll have to take a little time with it. The literal meaning of psychology is "science of the soul." But knowing that does not make any clearer to us precisely what this science of the soul is. What does it study? What are its methods? What are its goals?

Most people think psychology is a relatively modern science. They have that impression because it is essentially only in the last 100 to 150 years that the word "psychology" has come into use. But they forget that there was a premodern psychology that began—let us say—about 500 B.C. and continued into the seventeenth century. That psychology did not call itself "psychology," however. It was known as "ethics" or often as "philosophy," but that does not make it any the less psychology. What was the purpose of that premodern psychology? Our answer can be quite brief: *Premodern psychology sought to understand the human soul in the interest of making people better.* The motivation behind psychology was therefore moral. Indeed, we could even say religious, or spiritual.

I'll just mention briefly here some examples of that premodern psychology. Buddhism developed an extensive psychology that is highly complex and subtle. Aristotle wrote a psychological textbook, but he titled it *Ethics.* The Stoics produced a very interesting psychology, and some of you may be familiar with the *Meditations* of Marcus Aurelius. In Thomas Aquinas you will find a system of psychology from which you can probably learn more than you can from most modern textbooks. His discussions of such concepts as narcissism, pride, humility, modesty, inferiority complex, and many more are as interesting and profound as you will find anywhere. Spinoza, too, wrote a psychology and, like Aristotle, entitled it *Ethics.* Spinoza was probably the first great psychologist to recognize clearly the power of the unconscious when he said that we are all aware of our desires but we are not aware of the motives behind those desires. As we shall soon see, it was that observation that provided the basis many years later for Freud's depth psychology.

The modern period has seen the rise of a totally different psychology, which is on the whole not much more than a hundred years old. This psychology has a different purpose. Its goal is not to understand the soul so that we can become *better* human beings; its goal is—to state the case crudely—to understand the soul so that we can become *more successful* human beings. We want to understand ourselves and others so that we can take the upper hand in life, so that we can manipulate others, so that we can shape ourselves in ways that will favor our own advancement.

We can fully grasp the difference between the tasks of premodern and modern psychology only if we understand how much culture and the goals of society have changed. Now, I'm sure that by and large people in classical Greece or in the Middle Ages weren't all that much better than we are today. Their everyday behavior was probably even worse than ours. But despite that their lives were governed by an idea, and that idea was that just the business of earning one's daily bread was not enough to make life worth living. Life had to have a meaning, and much of that meaning lay in human growth, in the development of our human powers. And therein lay the relevance of psychology.

Modern man sees things differently. He is not as interested in *being* and *becoming* more as he is in *having* more. He wants a better job, more money, more power, more respect. But we know that more and more people are beginning to doubt whether goals like those will really make them happy. Word is getting around, and such doubt is perhaps nowhere more evident than in the United States, the richest and most economically advanced country in the world. But I do not want to go into this subject at length here. All I want to suggest is that the two different ideas about the goals of life set two different directions for psychology to take. Now I would like to give you a brief sketch of the history of modern psychology so that you will have some idea of its main tendencies.

Modern psychology had very modest beginnings. It set out to study memory, acoustic and visual phenomena, the association of ideas, and the psychology of animals. Wilhelm Wundt was perhaps the most important and influential figure in those early days of modern psychology. Psychologists then did not write for the general public, and they were not particularly well known. They wrote for their colleagues, and only a few "laymen" showed any interest in their work and publications.

That situation changed radically, however, and psychology started gaining in popularity when it shifted its focus to the motives behind human behavior. That field of inquiry has dominated psychology for the last fifty years. It concerns us all, of course, for we all want to know what it is that motivates us and why we act on the motives we do rather than on quite different ones. If psychology can promise us some clarity on those questions, then it can obviously be of great value to us. And so it was that motivational psychology became perhaps the most popular of all sciences, and in recent decades it has, if anything, gained in popularity rather than lost.

There are two principal schools in this popular psychology: instinct theory and behaviorism. Let me begin with a few words about instinct theory. That theory goes back to one of the greatest thinkers of the nineteenth century, Charles Darwin, who was among the earliest scientists to inquire into instinct as a motivating force in human beings. Using his work as a basis, others went ahead to develop a theory that we might sum up in this way: Every human action has a motive behind it, and in every case that motive is an independent and innate instinct. We are born with instincts in us just as animals are. If we are aggressive, the reason is our aggressive instinct. If we are servile, blame our servile instinct; if we are avaricious, our avaricious instinct; if we are jealous, chalk that up to our jealous instinct; if we enjoy cooperation, then that is our cooperative instinct at work. If we are quick to flee danger, that is our flight instinct, and so on and so forth. Indeed, if we tally up all the instincts the instinct theoreticians have come up with, the final count comes to about two hundred different instincts, each one of which will motivate a certain kind of human behavior, just as a key on a piano will, when pressed, produce a certain note.

The leading proponents of instinct theory were two Americans, William James and William McDougall. Now you may have the impression from the summary I have just given you that the instinct theory is a very simplistic and rather naive theory. That is by no means so. Using the foundation that Darwin had provided, those two men and others with them, all of whom were important and perceptive thinkers, built an extremely interesting edifice. Its only problem, in my opinion, is that it is not properly constructed. It is actually not a building at all but only a mental construct that has no basis in reality at all. The most recent important theory of instinct to achieve great popularity is that of Konrad Lorenz, who has traced human aggression back to a more or less innate aggressive instinct.

One weakness of instinct theory is its tendency to oversimplify. It is just too simple an answer to postulate an instinct for every single bit of human behavior, and such postulation doesn't really explain anything. All it says is that actions have motives, that different actions have their own distinct motives, and that those motives are innate. But none of that could be proved for most of the so-called instincts. There are a few—such as defensive aggression, flight, and also, to a certain degree, sexual behavior, though here we are even less sure of our ground—in which quasi-instinctive elements are present. But here we must not overlook the fact that learning, the influence of culture and society, can significantly modify even those innate drives, so much so that in both humans and animals subjected to such modification the drives may almost disappear or, on the other hand, become greatly accentuated.

The other weakness of the theory was that some instincts were strongly developed in some individuals and cultures yet almost nonexistent in others. There are, for example, primitive tribes that are extremely aggressive while others display practically no aggressiveness at all. The same has held true for individuals. If someone comes to a psychiatrist today and says, "Doctor, I'm so furious I'd like to kill everybody, my wife, my children, myself . . .," the psychiatrist does not say, "Aha, the aggressive instinct is very strong in this man." Instead, he makes a diagnosis more along these lines: "This man must be ill. This aggressiveness he is expressing, this hatred that has built up inside him, is a sign of illness." If the man's aggressiveness were motivated by instinct, it would be normal, natural behavior and not a symptom of illness.

We find, too—and this is very important—that the most primitive of peoples, the hunter-gatherers, the people at the very earliest beginnings of civilization, were the least aggressive of all human beings. If aggressiveness were innate, then it should have been most evident in the hunter-gatherers. In fact, just the opposite is true. It was the growth of civilization, starting about 4000 B.C.; it was the creation of large cities, kingdoms, hierarchies, armies; it was the invention of war, the invention of slavery—and I use the word "invention" deliberately here, because neither of those things occur in nature—it was all these things that provided breeding grounds for sadism, aggression, and the desire to subjugate and destroy, ills that never existed to anywhere near the same degree among primitive, prehistoric peoples.

It was those weaknesses in the instinct theory that prompted the *behaviorists* to propose a totally contrary view. They maintain that absolutely nothing is innate in us and that everything people do is the result of social conditions and of very clever manipulation on the part of society or of the family. The most famous and important advocate of this school today is B. F. Skinner, who says in his book *Beyond Freedom and Dignity* something we might paraphrase like this: "Concepts like freedom and dignity are pure fictions. They don't exist at all but are simply products of influencing human beings in such a way that they will think they want to be free. Neither a desire for freedom nor a sense of human dignity is inherent in human nature." Let me give you a simple example of the theory at work. Little Johnny won't eat his spinach. If his mother punishes him, she will not—as many parents know—get very far. And Skinner agrees that punishment is not the correct method. There should be no great lectures about spinach. It should simply be served. And if little Johnny nibbles at it, then his mother should give him a friendly smile and promise him an extra piece of cake. The next time spinach appears on the table, little Johnny will be more inclined to eat it. Once again he wins his mother's smile, and this time she gives him a piece of chocolate. And so things continue until little Johnny is conditioned, that is, until he has learned that he will get a reward if he eats his spinach. Who doesn't like rewards? And after a while Johnny will eat his spinach with real pleasure, preferring it to any other vegetable. Now it's true that things can work out just that way. Skinner has invested a great deal of effort in finding the cleverest ways to do this sort of thing. The reward is not automatically repeated every time, for instance. It is omitted once, then reintroduced. Many ingenious studies and experiments have been made to see how people can best be seduced, how rewards can be used to make them do what the person giving out the rewards wants them to do. Skinner is not interested in why the manipulator wants people to do what he asks them to do, for Skinner does not think that values can have any objective meaning.

If we reflect on the situation of a psychologist in his laboratory, then it is easy enough to understand Skinner's position. Whether the mice or rabbits eat or don't eat is not of much interest. The only thing of interest is whether one can induce them, with one method or another, to eat or not to eat. And since behaviorists regard human beings too, themselves included, as guinea pigs, they are not interested in the question of why and to what end they condition others. They are interested in only two things: whether they can condition someone and how they can do it best. The

71

behaviorist separates human *behavior* from *human beings*. He does not study people in the process of behaving; he studies only the product, and the product is behavior. The human being who generates that behavior is expressly put to one side. Human beings as such are unimportant; they are the subject of philosophy, of speculation. What interests the behaviorist is what people *do*. He chooses to ignore the question of why such astonishingly large numbers of people do not react the way they should react if the theory were correct. He is not disturbed by the fact that many people rebel, refuse to conform, do not fall for the subtle bribes that are ultimately the essence of this whole theory. The theory assumes that most people prefer to be bribed rather than to be themselves and to realize the potential of their own natures and talents.

Instinct theory and behaviorism have one thing in common despite the great differences between them. Neither allows human beings the slightest control over their own lives. Instinct theory sees man driven by impulses that lie far back in his human and animal past. Behaviorism sees man driven by whatever social constructs and conditions happen to be in effect. He is as dominated by the opportunistic and seductive tricks of his society as the man of instinct is by the history of his species. But neither of the two, neither human model as proposed by the two theories, is based on what man actually wants, what he is, what is in accordance with his nature.

The two major schools account for the greater part of what goes by the name of "modern psychology" today. And I should add that behavioristic psychology is by far the more influential of the two. Most psychology professors at American universities are behaviorists, and Soviet psychology follows very similar paths for obvious political reasons.

Sigmund Freud's Three Basic Concepts

Along with the two schools of psychology we have just discussed there is a third, which was founded by Sigmund Freud and is known as psychoanalysis or depth psychology. Freud's goal was to achieve a rational understanding of human emotions, particularly the irrational ones. He wanted to understand what the causes or breeding grounds were for hate, love, submissiveness, destructiveness, envy, jealousy—for all the emotions that the great writers (take Shakespeare or Balzac or Dostoevski, for example) have treated so incisively in their plays and novels. Freud wanted to make all those emotions the subject of scientific inquiry. He created the science of the irrational. He wanted to make use of rational, not artistic, powers to understand the irrational. But it is nonetheless understandable that artists, particularly of the surrealistic school, were much more receptive to Freud's theory than were the psychologists and psychiatrists, who were ready to dismiss all such ideas as pure nonsense. Freud's approach was identical with the artist's: What are the human emotions and how can we understand them? All the psychiatrists wanted to know was how people can be cured of symptoms that either cause them pain or interfere with their adjustment to society and with their own success in life.

It is important to note here that Freud's purpose was not limited to a scientific investigation of the motives (that is, the emotions) behind human behavior. Unlike the advocates of the main schools of modern psychology, Freud shared premodern psychology's moral purpose. He wanted human beings to be able to understand themselves, to discover their unconscious, so that they could achieve independence. His goal was a rule of reason, the destruction of illusion. He wanted to see people become free and mature. His moral goals were those of the Enlightenment, of rationalism. But those goals went beyond what other psychologists set as their own goals or understood the goals of their field to be. The only goal those psychologists set themselves was to help people function better. The human model that Freud envisioned as his goal coincided in many respects with that projected by the great philosophers of the Enlightenment.

Freud's theory and his mode of expressing it were, however, strongly influenced by the spirit of his times, which is to say that the influence of Darwinism, materialism, and instinctivism is evident in his work. As a consequence his theory is sometimes couched in language that makes him appear to be an instinctivist, and great misunderstandings have resulted from that. What I would like to do now is outline for you what I consider to be the essence of Freud's discoveries. In doing so, I will be presenting my own personal view, which the majority of psychoanalysts do not share.

The first central concept I want to mention is that of the unconscious or of *repression*. This concept is usually forgotten today. When people think of psychoanalysis, the first things that come to their minds are the ego, the superego, and the id; the Oedipus complex; and the theory of libido, none of which Freud included in his basic definition of psychoanalysis.

So let us begin with repression. We often act on motives of which we are completely unconscious. A little example will show what I mean. Not long ago I received a visit from a colleague who I know does not particularly like me. Indeed, I was rather amazed that he wanted to come see me at all. He rang the doorbell; I opened the door; he held out his hand and said cheerfully: "Goodbye." Translation: His unconscious mind was already wishing he could be gone. He had not been looking forward to this visit, and he revealed that by saying "goodby" instead of "hello." What could either of us do? Nothing at all. Being a psychoanalyst himself, he realized that he had given himself away. He couldn't apologize by saying: "That isn't what I meant to say." That would have been hopelessly naive, for we both knew that what a psychoanalyst does with a slip of the tongue is see what it really reveals, not try to make it mean something else after the fact. The situation could be nothing but embarrassing, and we both said nothing. That is just one example of the kind of thing that happens hundreds of times, and Freud built his theories on the basis of many such examples.

Or take another example: a sadistic father who beats his son. I think it occurs less often today than fifty years ago, but let's take this example: a sadistic father, a man who takes pleasure in causing others pain or in exercising strict control over them. If you should ask him why he does what he does (and ordinarily you won't have to bother asking, because such people are usually quite willing to volunteer the information), he will say: "I have to do it so that my son will become (or remain) a decent person. I do it out of love for him." Do you believe that? Maybe, and then again maybe not. But just look at his face. Notice his expression when he gives his son a whipping. You'll see strong emotion in his eyes. What you will see is the face of a man who is full of hate and at the same time full of joy at being able to beat another human being. The same quality turns up in policemen (not, of course, all of them), in nurses, in prison guards, and in any number of private relationships. Such people will hide this quality more or less, depending on how much self-interest demands that they hide it. But let's go back to our example of the sadistic father. If we see him in action, we know that his motive is not what he claims it is. It is not his son's wellbeing that interests him. That is a "rationalization." His real motive is his sadistic impulse, but he is totally unaware of that.

Or take an example of much greater historical importance: Adolf Hitler. In his conscious mind Hitler always assumed he wanted only what was best for Germany: Germany's greatness, Germany's vitality, Germany's position of power in the world, and who knows what all. Although he issued the cruelest of orders, he never clearly felt—as far as we can tell—that he acted out of cruelty. He always felt he was acting out of a desire to help Germany. He was acting to make manifest the laws of history; he was acting in the name of fate, in the name of race, in the name of Providence. He was not aware that he was a man who enjoyed destruction. He couldn't bear the sight of dead soldiers or destroyed buildings. That's why he never visited the front during World War II. The explanation is not personal cowardice on his part but rather a reluctance to see the concrete consequences of his own lust to destroy. We observe a similar phenomenon in people who wash compulsively. Their conscious desire is to be clean all the time. But when we analyze such individuals, we find that they know, in their unconscious minds, that they have blood or filth on their hands. They want to free themselves from what they are unconsciously carrying about with them: a crime, perhaps only a potential one, a criminal intent they have to be constantly washing away. Hitler himself had something of that quality. He was not a compulsive washer, but many observers noticed that he was fastidious beyond the limits of normal cleanliness.

What I have meant to do with this example is simply to show the parallel to the sadistic father. Hitler did not want to own up to the reality of his destructive impulses. Instead, he repressed them and admitted only his good intentions. That was possible, of course, only up to a certain point. When he finally realized that Germany—or, more accurately—that he himself had lost the war, the repression of his destructive urge ceased. Suddenly he wanted to destroy all of Germany, the entire German people. He said in his own mind: "Because this nation was unable to win the war, it does not deserve to survive." And so at the very end this man's pure lust for destruction was fully revealed. It had always been present, had always been part of his character, but it had remained repressed and rationalized until, one day, there was no keeping it secret any longer. And even then he had to fabricate still another rationalization: "The Germans will have to die because they don't deserve to live."

Examples like this—dramatic ones and undramatic ones—can be found everywhere every day. People remain unaware of their real motives because, for any number of reasons, they cannot bear to know things about themselves that either go against their own consciences or against public opinion. If they became aware of their real motives, they would find themselves in a very uncomfortable situation. And so they prefer to remain unconscious of those things and not to come into conflict with what they regard as their "better selves" or with what most "respectable people" think.

Now we come to a very interesting consequence of repression and to the second of Freud's key concepts. If we make people conscious of the real motives behind their actions, they react with what Freud called *resistance*. They reject the information. Even information offered them in their own interests and with the best of will is violently rejected. They refuse to see this reality in themselves. They do not respond to this information the way the driver of an automobile would, for example, if someone else tells him his door isn't shut tight or his headlights aren't working. The driver is grateful for that information. Not so the people whom we make aware of their repressed motives. They respond with resistance. In all the cases of repression I have just mentioned we would expect that the individuals involved would put up resistance if we were to explain to them what was really going on inside them, if we told them what their inner reality was as opposed to the fiction they have built up about themselves.

How do people showing resistance behave? A typical reaction is anger, rage, aggression. When people hear what they do not want to hear, they become angry. They want, as it were, to wipe out the witness to their crimes. They can't very well kill him— that's a bit too risky—so they dispose of him in a symbolic way. They blow up and say, "You're speaking out of jealousy, out of some base motive. You hate me. You get pleasure out of saying nasty things about me." And so on. Sometimes they become so angry that they can become positively dangerous. To what extent they show their anger will depend on the circumstances. If it is not politic to show anger (as in the case of a subordinate and his chief), then the individual will probably prefer to say nothing and will wait until he goes home, where he may then vent his anger on his wife. But when there are no such constraints, as, for example, when the offended individual is the boss himself, then he can respond to the criticism of a subordinate (and we are always speaking here of criticism that is correct and hits the mark) in as high-handed a manner as he likes. The boss can rub in the subordinate's inferiority, or he can simply fire the subordinate. And of course the chief does not fire him with any awareness that the subordinate has wounded him—how, after all, could such a mere underling ever harm the boss? He fires him instead with the rationalization that this little man is a slanderer, a mean-spirited person.

Another and simpler method a person can use to put up resistance is to ignore what he does not want to hear. Unwelcome information will often be either misunderstood or completely ignored, particularly if it comes in the form of a brief remark that can be pushed aside or if the speaker delivering it does not insist on being heard. It is not always possible to turn a deaf ear, but doing so still remains the simplest and most common form of resistance.

Another form is exhaustion or depression. That is the route many marriage partners take with each other. When one partner says something that reveals the true motives behind the other's actions, the accused partner sinks into gloom and resignation and may then retaliate, silently or explicitly, with an accusation of his own: "Just look what you've done. Now I'm depressed again because of that remark you made." Whether the remark is true or not is of no importance. But whichever partner made the remark will soon learn to refrain from unearthing the other's unconscious motives again. He knows that he'll pay dearly if he does.

Another form resistance can take is running away. This often happens in marriages when we feel that our partner has discovered something we would rather keep hidden. We may not even be aware that a game of hide-and-seek is going on, but then one of us feels that the other is seeing more than we are. We can't put up with that; we don't want to grant the other's insight any validity, because we don't want to change. We want to stay the way we are, so the only solution is to go away. The same thing happens frequently in psychoanalysis. Patients will often break off treatment if the analyst says something they don't want to hear. And then the patient is likely to say: "I quit treatment because the analyst is crazy himself. He said things about me that prove he's crazy. How could anyone but a madman have said things like that?" Everyone else will see that the analyst was quite correct, but the person directly affected, who is terrified of working any changes in himself, can respond only with violence (and all the modes of resistance we have discussed here are forms of violence): "Get out of my sight. I don't want to hear that ever again."

The picture is entirely different when a person is ready for change. When he is ready to understand himself, when he is ready to know the real truth about himself so that he can begin to change, then he will tend to react not with anger or by running away. He will be grateful that someone will tell him what he needs to know for the sake of his own growth. He will be as grateful as he would be to a physician who diagnoses an illness for him. But most people are not intent on changing. All they want is proof that it is not they but everyone else who should change.

It is no exaggeration to say that most people invest the greater part of their energies in repression and then in resistance if repressed material is called to their attention. That is, of course, an incredible waste of energy, and it prevents many people from making fruitful use of their capabilities.

Now we come to the third of Freud's concepts, which is *transference*. In his narrow definition of transference, Freud meant the tendency of a patient to perceive the analyst as a personage from his early childhood, as his father or mother. The patient's reaction to the analyst is therefore not appropriate to the person who is actually sitting across from him or behind him. The patient sees the analyst as someone else (father or mother or possibly a grandparent) and ascribes to the analyst the role that personage played in his childhood. Let me cite an example that vividly illustrates this point. An analyst once told me about a female patient who had been coming to see him for three weeks. As she was about to leave his office one day, she looked at him closely and said, "What? You don't have a beard?" The analyst had never worn a beard. For three weeks she had thought he had a beard, because her father had worn a beard. The analyst was a cipher for her. Not even visually had she perceived him as a real human being. As far as she was concerned, he was her father, and therefore he had a beard.

But the concept of transference has significance far beyond its application in psychoanalytical therapy. Transference is probably one of the most common reasons for human *error and conflict* in sizing up reality. It makes us see the world through the glasses of our own wishes and fears and consequently makes us confuse illusion with reality. We do not see other people as they really are but the way we want them to be or fear that they are. Those illusions about other people take the place of reality. We do not perceive others as they are but as they appear to us to be, and when we react to them, we are reacting not to real human beings in their own right but to products of our imagination.

Now let's look at a few examples. Take two people who fall in love. This happens less frequently than it used to, because there are simpler means for achieving the same ends these days, but I don't want to get sidetracked on that issue. So let's assume that two people fall genuinely in love. They are totally overwhelmed by the beauty, the virtues, the noble qualities of the other and are hugely attracted to each other. All this may lead to marriage, but then, six months later, both partners discover that they are not married to the person they fell in love with. This is somebody else altogether. They had both fallen in love with phantoms, with transference objects. They saw in the other only what they wanted to see, goodness, cleverness, honesty perhaps, or perhaps qualities their mothers or fathers had had. And they had not noticed that they were dealing in illusion. Then what often happens is that both partners wind up hating each other, because they feel their partner has disappointed them. But what they have both really done is deceive themselves; they saw only illusion and not reality. But things do not have to happen that way; they should not happen that way. And in fact they would not happen that way if people would only learn to understand transference.

The same phenomenon can be observed in the realm of politics. Consider for a moment the kind of wild enthusiasm that millions upon millions of people can develop for political leaders (it has happened not only in Germany but in other countries as well). Sometimes those leaders have been bad; sometimes they have been good. That, however, is not the key question here, important though that question may be. More significant for our discussion is the fact that most people—and perhaps we should say "Thank God" here, although the tendency is also extremely dangerous—have a deep longing for someone who will come along and save the world, someone who will speak the truth, who will make us safe, who will lead, who means well by us. And when someone comes along who knows how to play the part of this well-meaning leader, then people transfer their expectations onto him and are convinced that he is their savior, their redeemer, even when he is in fact a destroyer who will bring catastrophe down on them and on their country. Even minor leaders often exploit people's expectations. Many politicians make deliberate and conscious use of the people's tendency for transference and achieve great successes by doing so. They manage to impress the voters because they have a good TV presence, because they tell people what they want to hear, because they kiss babies, and because they reinforce the illusion that they mean well. After all, if they like little children they can't be all bad.

None of this would happen if people understood more about transference, if they took the trouble to notice when their own expectations color what they see and when they perceive things impartially, if they would finally try to be a bit *critical*. Sometimes small, seemingly insignificant actions are more revealing than a person's major speeches or what he chooses to emphasize about himself. If all of us could learn to see through the illusions born of transference, our loves, our marriages, and our political lives could be essentially freed of a great curse; they could be freed of the confusion between reality and fictitious images. It not easy to distinguish between those two things. It requires study; it requires daily practice. Our everyday lives offer us an ample field for such practice. Also, along with the many disadvantages it has, television offers us one great advantage: It is very revealing of human character, because it allows us to observe faces, gestures, and expressions at close range. We can learn a great deal about a political leader by watching him and hearing him speak on television. But we won't learn much about him unless we have developed our powers of observation. From everything I have been saying here we can see how important an understanding of transference could be in improving the quality of our personal and political lives.

Further Developments in Psychoanalysis

The diverse schools of psychoanalysis, their development, and their future prospects can, I think, be summarized quite briefly. Sigmund Freud himself was the first to carry the development of psychoanalysis further. In the 1920s he began revising his old theory, which was based on the conflict between the sexual drive and the instinct for self-preservation, and developing a new theory, which was based instead on the conflict between two biological impulses: eros and the death wish. The one moves people to come together, to love; the other moves them to destroy. I can't go into the full significance of that development here, but what it in fact amounted to—although Freud did not see it that way—was a fundamental shift. We might even call it the beginnings of a new school of psychoanalysis, with Freud himself as its founder.

The second important development in psychoanalysis was the work of Carl Gustav Jung. Jung (like most other psychoanalysts who diverged from Freud and his ideas) did not ascribe to sexuality the central role that Freud gave it. Jung conceived of psychic energy as a unit and did not limit the term "libido" to sexual energy alone but identified it with psychic energies in general. With brilliant and profound insight, he showed that what psychoanalysts dredged up from the unconscious of their patients had its parallels in the mythologies and symbols of peoples all over the world, and in his investigations Jung included not only the most primitive of peoples but also cultures totally different from our own.

Alfred Adler took a different approach. His interest was not in myth and the depths of the psyche but rather in the strategy of the struggle for existence. He therefore regarded the will to power as the key concept for understanding human motivation. But to state Adler's case so baldly is to oversimplify him grossly. His writings are extraordinarily intelligent and complex, and he contributed a great deal to our understanding of human nature. He was also the first psychoanalyst—and here he was way ahead of Freud—to give human aggression a central place in his psychological system.

There are two other schools that deserve mention here and that have much in common with each other. The first is the psychiatric school founded by the Swiss-born American psychiatrist Adolf Meyer; the second is the work of Harry Stack Sullivan, one of the most outstanding American psychoanalysts. The English psychologist Ronald D. Laing has built on Sullivan's insights, following them through to their most radical and, in my opinion, their most fruitful consequences. Despite all the differences that separate them, these men are in agreement on two main points. First, they reject the idea that sexuality is the mainspring of all human behavior. Second, they focus instead on interpersonal relationships, on what goes on among people, on how they influence each other and react to each other, on the makeup of the field that is created when human beings live together. Interestingly enough, these psychoanalysts have concentrated their attention on schizophrenia, which they do not basically regard as an illness in the usual sense of that word. They see it instead as the result of personal experience, of interpersonal relationships that have had clearly drastic consequences but essentially add up to no more than another psychological problem like any other psychological problem. Laing has made particularly fruitful use of that theory, because he has been able to see more clearly than anyone else the relationship of schizophrenia as an individual "illness" to the social situation not only within the family but also within society.

A number of other psychoanalysts have developed similar positions. The theories of Fairbank, Guntrip, and Balint, as well as my own work, take this same point of departure. They focus primarily, however, not on schizophrenia but rather on the social and ethical forces at work in the formation of interpersonal relationships.

Now that we have taken a look at the development of psychoanalysis and at its most significant achievements, one more important question remains to be considered. What does the future of psychoanalysis look like? I would like to attempt to answer that question, but to do so is not easy, because opinions are sharply divided on the subject. We can begin to circumscribe it perhaps by citing two extreme positions. The first claims that psychoanalysis is useless, that it has no successes to its credit, that attempts to help people with psychoanalysis are exercises in futility. The other extreme claims that analysis is the cure and solution for all psychic problems; if someone is having problems, then what he should do is stretch out on the couch and submit to three or four years of analysis. Until not too long ago that was a commonly held view in America, but the emergence of other therapies has done much to weaken it in recent years.

The claim that analysis has no healing effects whatsoever is, in my opinion, untenable. It is not substantiated by my own forty years of experience as an analyst or by the experience of many of my colleagues. We should also keep in mind here that in many cases analysts are not as competent as they should be (no profession is immune to that) and that the selection of patients is often not fortunate. Attempts are often made to analyze patients for whom the method is not suitable. The truth is that analysis has cured many people of their symptoms, and it has helped many others achieve clarity about themselves for the first time, has helped them be more honest with themselves, to be somewhat freer, to live closer to reality. That is in itself an extremely worthwhile achievement and one that is often grossly undervalued.

There are, of course, certain trends of the times that partially account for the turn against analysis. Many people feel that medicine is the only thing that is of real help. If there's nothing we can swallow, then there's no help for us. Pills are the great cure-all. Another prevailing view is that we ought to be able to cure everything and anything overnight. We find this view represented in T. A. Harris's book *I'm Okay, You're Okay,* an altogether superficial book with the obligatory smattering of Freudian theory. It may be of some help if people believe in it, just as any suggestion people believe in can "help." What the book offers can be done quickly, is simple, requires no thought, and, worst of all, does not demand that we deal with our own resistance. This is the key point that therapy of this kind avoids. Everything should be made simple; everything should be made easy. That's the trend of the times. People think we should be able just to swallow everything as easily as we can a pill. And if learning something requires effort, then it's not worth learning.

There's a story that can illustrate what I mean here. A young man goes into an elegant restaurant, asks for a menu, studies it for a long time, and says to the headwaiter, "I'm sorry, but you don't have anything I like." Then he gets up and leaves. Two weeks later he comes back, and the headwaiter asks—very politely, because this is a very high-class restaurant—why he couldn't find anything he liked the last time. The young man replies, "Oh, I could have found something all right, but my analyst told me I should practice being assertive." With that method we can learn to be more sure of ourselves, can learn how to appear more confident, how to lose our fear of headwaiters, and so on. But what we don't learn is *why* we are so insecure. We remain ignorant of the fact—and here we touch on the theme of transference again—that we tend to regard everyone else as an authority, as a father figure. Even if the method does yield some quick results in the restaurant and we feel a little more self-confident, we still have not gotten to the root causes of our insecurity at all, and behind our new façade we remain the same insecure people we always were. Indeed, our situation is even worse than it was, for we are no longer aware that we are insecure. And why are we insecure?

Not because we are afraid of authority but because we are not fully developed human beings, because we lack the strength of our convictions, because we have remained small children who hope others will help us, because we have not grown up, because we are full of self-doubt, and so on. The methods of behavioristic therapy can't help in cases like that. All they do is sweep the dirt under the rug.

But not all criticism of psychoanalysis is unjustified. I'd like to mention a few objections to it that I consider quite sound. Psychoanalysis can often degenerate into mere chatter. Freud's idea of free association is in part responsible for this. In encouraging the patient to say anything that occurred to him, Freud assumed that the patient would say those things that came from his depths, things that were genuine and of real importance. But in many analyses patients simply babble away and run down their husbands for the hundredth time or complain about everything their awful parents did to them. Nothing comes of that. They go over the same ground again and again. But—someone is listening. The patient feels that the fact of someone listening helps somehow and that his situation will eventually improve. But that kind of talk alone never changed anyone or anything. It is not what Freud had in mind. His method involved discovery and struggle against resistance. Freud never assumed that we could achieve anything, much less solve difficult psychic problems, without expending effort. Without effort we can't attain any of our goals in life, no matter what the advertisements may claim to the contrary. Anyone who fears effort, anyone who backs off from frustration and possibly even pain will never get anywhere, especially not in analysis. Analysis is hard work, and analysts who gloss that over harm their own cause.

Another failing in many analyses is emphasizing intellectualization over emotion. The patient theorizes endlessly about the significance of the time his grandmother hit him or some other such incident. And if he has an especially strong academic streak, he may develop highly complicated theories; he may construct theory upon theory; *but he will feel nothing.* He does not feel what is inside him. He does not feel his fear. He does not feel his inability to love, his isolation from others. His resistance makes all that inaccessible to him. And so analysis may fall in step with the times in giving precedence to *cerebral man,* the purely rational human being. We expect intelligence to take care of everything; emotion is only useless ballast that we ignore as much as possible.

And finally I would like to say that there are too many people who think they have to run to a psychoanalyst the minute they encounter the least little difficulty in their lives. They don't even try to cope with their problems themselves. People should go to a psychoanalyst only if they find that their own best efforts have still left them unable to understand and improve their situation themselves.

Analysis remains the best therapy for a number of disorders having to do with excessive preoccupation with self or, in other words, with narcissism, which in turn results in an inability to relate to others. No other method is as effective and fruitful for treating flight into illusion, stalled psychic growth, symptoms like compulsive washing, and any number of other symptoms of an obsessive or compulsive nature.

Psychoanalysis also serves another function that is at least as important as its curative one. It can aid in promoting psychic growth and self-realization. I'm sorry to say that only a small minority seem to be interested in psychic growth these days. Most people have an entirely different goal, which is to own more and consume more. When they reach twenty, they assume that their growth is complete, and from then on they direct all their energies to making the best possible use of this completed machine. As they see it, it would work to their disadvantage if they were to change; for if a person changes then he no longer fits the pattern that he and others expect him to fit. If he changes, how can he know whether he will still hold the same opinions ten years from now that he holds now? And how would a change like that affect his ability to get ahead? Most people do not want to grow and change, do not want to realize themselves. They want to hang onto the options they have, exploit them, "capitalize" on them.

There are, of course, exceptions to that rule. There are counter-movements, particularly in the United States. Many people have come to realize that even if we own and enjoy all manner of things we can still be unfulfilled and unhappy, that life can still be meaningless, that we can remain depressed and anxious. "What meaning can life have," we ask ourselves, "if our only purpose in it is to buy a somewhat more expensive car the next time around?" People have seen how their parents or grandparents sacrificed their entire lives to the acquisition of the things they thought they wanted. With varying degrees of clarity, this minority has rediscovered a piece of ancient wisdom: Man does not live by bread alone; possessions and power do not guarantee happiness but tend instead to create anxiety and tension. These people want to pursue a different goal. They want to *be* more rather than *have* more. They want to be more rational, to rid themselves of illusions, and to change social conditions that can be maintained only with the aid of illusion. That longing often takes rather naive forms, such as enthusiasm for Oriental religion, for yoga, for Zen Buddhism, and so on. My use of the word "naive" does not apply to those religions, which are not naive at all, but to the way the new enthusiasts approach them. They are taken in by the advertising of a few Indian fakirs who pass themselves off as holy men and by all manner of groups that claim they know how to cultivate human sensitivity. Here, I feel, psychoanalysis has an important mission. It can help us understand ourselves, perceive our own reality, free ourselves from illusion, free ourselves, too, from the grip of anxiety and greed. It can make us capable of perceiving the world differently. Once we can forget the *self* as the prime focus of our interest and once we experience ourselves as acting, feeling, nonalienated human beings, then the world becomes the prime focus of our interest, our concern, our creative energies.

We can practice those attitudes. And psychoanalysis can help us in this practice, because it is a method that helps us experience ourselves as we really are, helps us experience who we are, where we stand, where we are going. It is therefore advisable to work with a psychoanalyst who understands those connections and does not think the purpose of analysis is to help people adjust and conform. But that kind of analysis should not go on too long; overly extensive analysis often creates dependencies. Once a patient has learned enough to make use of the tools himself, he should begin analyzing himself. And that is a lifelong task that we carry on until the day we die. We can best practice self-analysis the first thing each morning, combining it with the kind of breathing and concentration exercises used in Buddhist meditation. The important thing is to step back from the bustle of life, to come to ourselves, to stop reacting constantly to stimuli, to make ourselves "empty" so that we can become active within ourselves.

Anyone who attempts this will, I think, experience a deepening of his capacity to feel; he will experience "healing," a recovery of health, not in the medical sense but in a profound, human sense. But this process requires patience, and patience is certainly not a commodity we have in great abundance. To any and all who want to make the attempt, though, I wish the best of luck.

In the Name of Life:
A Portrait Through Dialogue

SCHULTZ: What we propose here is a conversation, not an interview. Ours will be an unprepared, unpremeditated, impromptu conversation without any set theme or purpose, talk for the sake and pleasure of talk alone.

When I think about my role in our joint enterprise, I see myself as a reader visiting with an author whose books he has read, a reader who would like to learn a bit more than he could find on the printed page. I hope to spend most of my time this evening listening, and what I would like to do is not subject you to an interrogation but ask a few questions that will encourage you to speak.

That sounds a bit old-fashioned and smacks a bit of the drawing room, even though we're in a broadcasting studio. People don't ordinarily converse in studios. They either hold discussions or manufacture entertainment, produce it for mass consumption, like any other commodity, without worrying about what may be true or untrue. But for us tonight, interest in the truth will be at the heart of our conversation.

Our word "conversation" derives from the same Latin root as "conversion" does, and the possibility of a conversion, of a "turning around," is always inherent in any true conversation, for when we converse we take part in a game in which exchange, not victory, is the goal, an intellectual game in which no one stars and everyone wins.

So much for the preliminaries. Now I would like to ask you, Professor Fromm, whether you feel what we are doing here has any real place in our times or not. Who, except for a few eccentrics, would ever want to revive something that is clearly on its way out and that, at best, is generally regarded as a holdover from the past? We are witnessing the quiet demise of the art of letter writing. Can we still rescue the art of conversation? I fear we cannot, and I find that—to put it mildly—a great pity.

FROMM: I would go a step further and call it a dreadful shame, for it is symptomatic of a defect in our culture that is not only regrettable but may also prove lethal. Perhaps I can put what I mean this way: We find ourselves giving more and more of our time and energy to things that have a point, that produce results. And when all is said and done, what are those results? Money, perhaps, or fame or a promotion. We hardly ever consider doing something any more that has no purpose. We've forgotten that it is possible, even desirable and, above all, pleasurable to do something without a specific goal in mind. One of life's greatest pleasures is to make use of our powers not to attain a goal but for the sake of an activity itself. Take love, for example. Love has no purpose, though many people might say: Of course it does! It is love, they say, that enables us to satisfy our sexual needs, marry, have children, and live a normal, middle-class life. That is the purpose of love. And that is why love is so rare these days, love without goals, love in which the only thing of importance is the act of loving itself. In this kind of love it is *being* and not *consuming* that plays the key role. It is human self-expression, the full play of our human capacities. But in a culture like ours, which is exclusively oriented to external goals like success, production, and consumption, we can easily lose sight of that kind of love. It fades so far into the distance that we can hardly even imagine it as a reality any more.

Conversation has become either a commodity or a way of doing battle. If the conversational battle takes place in the presence of a large audience, then it assumes the quality of a gladiatorial contest. The participants go for each other's throats, and each one tries to destroy the other. Or they converse merely to show how clever or superior they are. Or they converse to prove to themselves that they are in the right once again. Conversation is a way of demonstrating to themselves that what they happen to think is indeed correct. They go into conversation determined not to admit any new thoughts into their minds. They have their opinion. Each knows what the other will say. And all they demonstrate is that neither one can be moved from his position.

A genuine conversation is not a battle but an exchange. The question of who is right and who is wrong is completely beside the point. It doesn't even matter whether what the participants say is particularly cogent or profound. What matters is the genuineness of what they say. Let me give you a little example of what I mean. Suppose two people are on their way home together, two colleagues of mine, two psychoanalsts, and one of them says, "I'm kind of tired." And the other replies, "Me, too." Now that may sound like a rather banal exchange, but it isn't necessarily, for if these two people do the same kind of work, then they know just what the other's tiredness is like, and so they have engaged in genuine, human communication: "We're both tired, and we've each let the other know how tired we are." That is much more of a conversation than when two intellectuals start throwing big words around in a discussion of the lastest theory about this or that. They are simply holding two separate monologues and do not touch each other at all.

The art of conversation and joy in conversation (conversation in the sense of being open, being together, usually takes verbal form, but it can also take the form of movement in dancing; there are many ways to converse)—these things will become possible again only if major changes take place in our culture, that is, only if we can rid ourselves of our monomaniacal, goal-oriented way of life. We need to cultivate attitudes that recognize the *expression and full realization of human potential* as the only worthwhile goals in life. To put it in the simplest possible terms: What matters is *being* as opposed to *having,* to just using and consuming and getting ahead.

SCHULTZ: We have much more free time than we used to have and therefore more opportunity for conversation. But the more the external circumstances of our lives encourage it, the less internal inclination toward it we seem to have. There is too much that interferes with that being together you spoke of; there are too many gadgets and machines that get in our way. It seems that a very specific and pervasive attitude prevents us from engaging in what we have been calling "conversation" here.

FROMM: I think we could even say that many people (probably the great majority) are afraid of being left alone with each other without some plan of action, without a radio or TV, without a subject to discuss, without an agenda. They are afraid and feel totally lost. They have no idea what to say to each other. I don't know if this holds true in Germany, but in the United States it is customary never to invite a single individual or just one other couple to your home. You always have to have more guests, because it can be embarrassing if you are only four. In a small company you have to work hard to keep things from being boring, unless you plan to play all your old records. If you have a party of six, you still won't have any real conversation, but you'll at least avoid painful lulls in the chatter. Somebody will always have something to say. When one person runs out of subjects, someone else can step in. It's a kind of double concert. The music never stops, but no real conversation takes place.

I suspect a lot of people think that if a form of entertainment doesn't cost anything it can't be very satisfying. Industry propaganda has trained us all to think that happiness comes from objects that we can buy, and very few of us are ready to believe any more that we can live and live very happily without all that stuff. That is a great change from the past. I'm seventy-three now. Fifty years ago people bought very few things for their entertainment, even people with comfortable middle-class incomes. There was no radio or TV; there were no cars. But there was conversation. Of course, if you look upon conversation as a means of "diversion," then your conversation will be mere twaddle. Real conversation does not "divert." It requires concentration, a gathering of our powers, not a scattering of them. If a person is not alive within himself, then his conversation can't be very lively either. But there are many people who could be much livelier if they were not afraid to step out of themselves, to show who they really are, to cast off the crutches they think they need to keep from tumbling down into nothingness, if they were not afraid to be alone with themselves and others.

SCHULTZ: We are talking on the radio. It is radio and television's job to inform and entertain the public. That mission is codified in the laws governing broadcasting. But on the other hand, as you have suggested and as no one could possibly doubt, radio and television have contributed greatly to the demise of the art of conversation.

FROMM: That's a question that interests me a great deal. I'd very much appreciate hearing what your experience has been. Do you feel that radio and television have essentially the same effect on people and fulfill a similar function, or do you think these two media have very different functions and qualities?

SCHULTZ: I feel that they are very different, and when I say I feel that, I mean to suggest that I don't have much apart from my own hunches to go on. Scientific studies that have attempted to pin down the difference between the effects of radio and television have not as yet been able to turn up any solid results. So I'll respond to your question with just a few of my own subjective impressions and observations.

It seems to me that neither radio nor television is an agent of dialogue. They work indirectly. In both of them there is someone on the giving end and someone on the receiving end. There can be no contradictions, no back talk. When the radio or TV is turned on, conversation stops. Radio and TV can create the impression of conversation, but they can't really make it come about. That, I feel, is a privilege reserved for living human beings. The crucial issue is whether radio and television invite us, stimulate us, challenge *us* to converse or whether they are inimical to the conditions that make conversation possible. But in that regard radio seems less harmful to me than television.

Television encourages passivity, a comfortable consumer mentality, more than any other medium. It is the most successful means we have ever developed to help us "pass time." But real conversation demands time. If we pass our time and kill our time, conversation cannot flourish. Radio, if I'm seeing things right, does not exert so strong an attraction. It promotes and demands more alertness, more imagination. It could be, if it wanted to be, an inexhaustible source of material for conversation. It cannot offer conversation itself, but it can offer the stuff of conversation.It can point us toward other, more basic and direct means of communication, calling our attention, say, to the uniqueness and delight of face-to-face conversation.

FROMM: What you say certainly makes sense to me. All I have to go on here is my own personal experience as a radio listener and occasional watcher of TV. I've found, on comparing notes with my wife, that her reactions to radio and TV are similar to my own. I'd be curious to have your comments on our experience, and I'd also like to ask our listeners whether they respond to these two media the same way I do. I find that when I'm listening to the radio I'm still a free man. I turn it on when there's a program that interests me. *But I do not become addicted to it.* With the aid of radio technology, I can listen to a conversation somewhat in the same way that I listen to someone else speaking on the telephone. What I hear on the radio is not, of course, as personal as a telephone conversation, but the point I want to make is that we take both the radio and the telephone in stride. We are not fascinated by them, and so I can truly say that I am free either to listen to the radio or not listen to it. My reaction to television is quite different. With television I lose a bit of my freedom. The minute the set is turned on and I see the picture on it, I experience what I would hesitate to call a compulsion but what is certainly a strong impulse or inclination to watch, even if I know intellectually that the program is utter drivel. I do not mean to say that everything on television is drivel. All I want to suggest is that even when a show is utter drivel and even when I know that's what it is, I still feel drawn to watch it and listen to it.

Television holds a fascination far greater than that of radio. It exerts a kind of psychological spell that cannot be explained in terms of the content of any particular program. I've often asked myself what this fascination is, and I think it is rooted in some very profound level of our nature: By merely pressing a button, we can summon another world into our living rooms. That appeals to profound magical instincts.

With television I become a kind of god. I can get rid of the reality I actually live with, and in its place I can create a new reality that appears when I press the button. I'm almost God the Creator. The world I see is my world. That reminds me of a story that not only illustrates this point vividly but also has the advantage of being true. A father and his six-year-old son were riding in the family car on a rainy, stormy day. They had a flat tire and had to stop to change it. Given the weather, that was a thoroughly unpleasant task, and the boy said to his father, "Daddy, can't we change to a different channel?" That's the way the child saw the world. If this one doesn't suit me, I'll switch to another one.

My wife recently read a novel by a Polish author and then told me the story, which I found utterly intriguing. The novel tells about the son of a very wealthy and eccentric man. The boy grows up in a big house, but he is not taught how to read or write and he never speaks with another human being. He grows up in his parental house but in total isolation. All he has available to him is a television set. He leaves it on all day, and he thinks that what he sees on it is reality. Then his father dies. The son has to leave the house and go out among other people. But he never grasps that what he sees firsthand is a reality different from that of the television. The young man never says a word, can't say a word, because he knows nothing. All he can do is watch, because for him the world is nothing but a television show. But precisely because he says nothing and because he eventually winds up in the house of one of the most powerful men in America, people think he must be terribly important. Pretty soon everyone knows his name, and in the end he is nominated for president because he never says anything and hasn't any opinions at all.

This story illustrates just what I have been talking about. Reality and what we see in television have become one, and I think that this experience of being able to press a button and make another world become reality is—as you have said—a profound, atavistic experience and one that we find incredibly seductive. That is why television has no need, as it were, to offer anything "good." It's appeal lies in the very nature of the medium. People are drawn to it the way they are to a fire or to any other exciting spectacle—

SCHULTZ: —where they can remain spectators and are in no way prepared to take any action themselves. The flip side of this illusion of power (that can be had by pressing a button) is, then, total passivity. With radio, the possibility still remains (as Adam Müller once expressed it) that listening can be a kind of response, a predisposition to activity that should not be confused with merely waiting for enlightenment.

But now let me ask another question, Professor Fromm. You say you are in no position to judge the situation in Germany. But television has brought about drastic changes in our *listening* habits. Now that television has gotten people out of the habit of attending to anything fully and closely, we can no longer assume that we have our listeners' attention. What I want to ask you is this: Hasn't radio given in to this tendency too quickly? Hasn't it been too ready to accept the evidence or claims of those who say that attention is no longer available in great quantity? Shouldn't it somehow be fighting this tendency? Television has reduced radio to a more modest role. Indeed, radio hardly qualifies as a mass medium any more—a situation for which we should perhaps be grateful. Shouldn't radio therefore be defining new tasks for itself that will take into account these differences we have been discussing here?

FROMM: I can't speak with any authority here because I am not familiar enough with the offerings of German radio. But I do feel what you have said touches the heart of the matter. I know that South German Radio has offered an extensive series of programs covering subjects ordinarily treated in university courses. The language has been somewhat simpler perhaps, but that is all to the good. (It would be an improvement in our university courses if instructors used simpler language to convey more content.) This, it seems to me, is an admirable task for radio and one in which it can fill a significant educational role. And what you have said about concentration is extremely important, too. It is remarkable with how little concentration people think, live, and work these days. Work is so fragmented and shattered that concentration is usually only mechanical and partial. We rarely encounter that full concentration that involves the whole person. A worker on an assembly line who has to tighten the same screw over and over again needs a certain kind of concentration to keep up his pace, but this type of concentration is very different from the gathering together of all our powers that we find in true concentration. A person with real concentration is capable of listening without his thoughts wandering off; he will not try to do five things at once because he can't find any one thing that really satisfies him. And, of course, without concentration we can't accomplish anything. Everything we do without concentration will have little value. If concentration is lacking, our activities will not provide us or anyone else with satisfaction. That holds true for all of us, not just for great artists or scientists.

SCHULTZ: I'd like to interrupt our conversation for a moment here, Professor Fromm, to fill in our listeners on some of the particulars of your career.

Erich Fromm was born in Frankfurt on March 23, 1900. He was an only child. He grew up in the Jewish tradition, and I will be asking him some questions about that aspect of his background soon. The stories from the Old Testament—he tells us—made a powerful and lasting impression on him. As a boy he was particularly drawn to the vision of universal peace, to the vision of the lion and the lamb lying down together, and at an early age he developed a strong interest in internationalism and the communal life of nations. In his high school years the irrationality and mass hysteria that led to war in 1914 evoked revulsion and protest in him.

About that same time he had a personal experience crucial to his subsequent development. A beautiful young woman, an artist and a friend of his family, committed suicide after the death of her old, unprepossessing father. It was her last wish to be buried with him. The question this woman's death posed continued to gnaw at Fromm. How could she have loved her father so much that she chose death with him over the joys of life, joys that were accessible and familiar to her? That experience and the questions it raised led Fromm to the discipline of psychoanalysis. He began inquiring into the motives behind human behavior.

During his university studies he came upon some authors who might seem like strange bedfellows for the Old Testament prophets, whose writings Fromm knew by heart. Buddha, Marx, Bachofen, and Freud were the main intellectual influences to come into his life at that time. As different, perhaps even as antagonistic, as those authors may seem, Fromm managed to bring them together under one roof. But this, too, is a theme we will be discussing in more detail very soon, and I won't go into it any further here.

Fromm studied psychology, philosophy, and sociology in Heidelberg, taking his doctorate at the age of twenty-two. He continued to pursue his studies in Munich and Frankfurt. He concluded his training at the renowned Psychoanalytic Institute in Berlin, and in 1930 he became a practicing psychoanalyst. Apart from his work in Berlin, he taught at the Psychoanalytic Institute in Frankfurt and also became an instructor and member in the Institute for Social Research at the University of Frankfurt. That institute carried on its work at Columbia University in New York after the Nazis came to power in Germany. Fromm went to the United States himself in 1934. He taught at various universities, founded several important institutes for psychoanalysis and social psychology, and at the same time insisted on remaining a practicing analyst working directly with patients. In 1949 he accepted a post at the National University of Mexico, which awarded him an honorary professorship after his retirement in 1965. During his years in Mexico his work continued to be both varied and influential. In recent years he has been living in Tessin and concentrating on writing, although he also still does some teaching in both Mexico and New York.

Professor Fromm has long been active in the cause of peace and was one of the founders of SANE, a major American peace organization that, in addition to its work against the nuclear arms race, was also a leader in the protest against the Vietnam War. In the 1950s he joined a socialist party but then resigned from it because its goals did not seem radical enough to him. His work on incorporating psychoanalytic theory into Marxian social theory is of prime importance in that field and has gone hand in hand with his humanistically and socially oriented revision of Freudian theory. He edited the contributions that international scholars made to a symposium on socialistic humanism, and it would be difficult to find anyone else in his field who has given more attention to political problems. His book *Revolution of Hope* is a kind of polemical pamphlet that he wrote in support of Eugene McCarthy's candidacy for the presidency of the United States. Fromm backed the professorial Senator despite the fact—or I should say *because of* the fact—that McCarthy was a politician of philosophical and poetic tastes. What was so important for Fromm in McCarthy's candidacy was that McCarthy was able to awaken hope in his countrymen, and in Fromm's mind hope is an eminently political commodity. What is so striking about Professor Fromm—and this quality is by no means common in academics—is the unconventional, unorthodox view that comes through in everything he thinks, says, and does. What we find in him is not pale thought but an enlivening freshness. He sweeps away the dust. He opens up new avenues of inquiry. He abhors dogma and fixed positions.

In Hebrew, *spirit* and *wind* are represented by one and the same word. Precisely because he remains perennially unfinished, neither his friends nor his foes, neither his supporters nor his detractors, can pigeonhole him.

SCHULTZ: Professor Fromm, now that I've given this brief sketch of your career, may I ask you to tell us a bit about yourself? I once found the phrase "intellectual biography" in your work. What were the influences and impressions of your youth and student years that helped set the course of your life?

FROMM: A few things occur to me here that are perhaps worth mentioning. Being the only child of two overly anxious parents did not, of course, have an altogether positive effect on my development, but over the years I've done what I could to repair that damage.

Something that had a positive influence on me, or at least a decisive one, was my family heritage. I was born into a strictly Orthodox Jewish family with a long line of rabbinical forefathers on both sides. I grew up in the spirit of this old tradition, which was a prebourgeois, precapitalist tradition, a tradition that was certainly more medieval than it was modern. And that tradition had greater reality for me than the twentieth-century world I was living in. I attended a German school, of course, and went to a gymnasium. I then studied at the university and was profoundly affected by the ideas I drew from German culture, a point I'd like to come back to again a little later on.

My sense of the world, however, was not that of a modern man but of a premodern one; and that attitude was reinforced by studying the Talmud, reading the Bible a lot, and hearing a lot of stories about my ancestors, who had all lived in a world that predated the bourgeois world. Let me tell you a story to illustrate what I mean. One of my great-grandfathers was a great Talmudist, but he was not a rabbi. He had a small shop in Bavaria, and he earned very little money. Then one day he was offered a chance to earn more money if he would do a little traveling. He had a lot of children, and that didn't make his lot any easier. His wife said to him: "Maybe you should think about taking this opportunity. You'd be gone only three days a month, and we'd have a little more money." And he said: "Do you think I should do that and lose more than three days of study a month?" She replied: "For God's sake, of course not!" And that was the end of that. So my great-grandfather sat in his shop and studied the Talmud. Whenever a customer came in, he would look up and snap at him: "Isn't there some other shop you can go to?" That was the world that was real to me. I found the modern world strange.

SCHULTZ: For how long?

FROMM: Until today. I recall that when I was ten or twelve whenever someone told me he was a salesman or businessman I always felt a little embarrassed. I'd think to myself: God, he must feel awful having to admit that he's not doing anything else with his life except earning money. Imagine, having nothing else to do! In the meantime I've learned that that's quite normal. But it still surprises me. I've remained an alien in the business or bourgeois culture, and that explains why I developed such a harshly critical attitude toward bourgeois society and capitalism. I became a socialist. The society I saw and the interests it had did not reflect what I thought life was all about. But that required no great intellectual decision on my part. I had always found the normal state of affairs alien to me and wondered how such an order could ever have come about.

SCHULTZ: But surely you had experiences that ran counter to this basic feeling, too; for no one could very well claim that the modern world has no place in your thinking and your life. On the contrary, it is very powerfully present, both with its dangers and with its signs of hope.

FROMM: My answer to that can be quite simple. What attracted me to the modern world was everything in it that pointed back to the prebourgeois past. There was Spinoza. There was Marx. There was Bachofen. With them I felt at home. In them I found a synthesis between the things of the past that were still alive for me and the things of the modern world that I loved. The aspects of the modern world that had their roots in the old felt close to me, and that's why I experienced no contradiction between those two worlds. Such was the world I was familiar with, the world I enjoyed, and so I became an eager student of everything that created this link between the old and the new.

SCHULTZ: Did this happen during your student years or earlier? When did these two worlds meet in your consciousness?

FROMM: As you mentioned earlier, World War I was a crucial event in my development. I was fourteen when the war broke out. Like most of the boys in my class, I was still a child then, and I didn't really understand what the war was all about. But it wasn't long before I began to see through all the supposed justifications for it, and so I started to puzzle over a question that has pursued me for the rest of my life. Or perhaps I should say I have pursued it: *How is this possible?* How is it possible that millions of people can kill millions of other people, that they let themselves be killed, that it can take four years before an end can be called to this inhuman situation? And all that for goals that are in part quite obviously irrational and for political notions that no one would sacrifice his life for if he could only see them for what they are. How is war *politically* possible, and how is war *psychologically* possible? Those became burning questions for me at the time, and they have remained the questions that have influenced my thinking more than any others right up to the present day. My prebourgeois background and World War I were probably the two factors that formed my thinking and sensibility more than any other.

SCHULTZ: What books contributed to your orientation? And I don't mean just books directly related to your professional training but also books that have shaped your personal life.

FROMM: I've given that question a lot of thought myself. There are in fact a few books that have formed my life, that have, if you will, "inspired" me. And if I may insert a footnote here, I'd like to say that I think there ought to be books that set the tone of our lives. Most of what we read does not have that power. It either falls within the province of our special field, or it has no meaning for us at all. But every one of us should ask himself: Is there one book, are there two or three books that have been absolutely central to your entire development?

SCHULTZ: If I may interrupt for just a second, there's a remark of Flaubert's that seems very much to the point here: "I read not to learn but to live."

FROMM: Exactly! That's a wonderful quote. I hadn't heard it before, but it expresses perfectly what I want to say. Seen by that standard, there aren't many books that are truly influential for us. Any half-way decent book will, of course, have some effect on us. No book leaves us completely untouched, any more than a serious conversation or meeting with another person does. If two people speak seriously together they will both experience something, or—as I prefer to put it—they will both undergo a change. The change will often be so minute that we can't detect it. But this line of thought takes us back to the point you mentioned earlier: If two people talk together and both of them remain the same people they were before, then they haven't really talked at all. They have simply engaged in an exchange of words.

The same is true of books. There have been three, four, five books in my life that have made me what I am. What I would have become without them I can't say. First of all come the books of the prophets. Notice that I do not say the "Old Testament." When I was young, I did not detest the military accounts of the conquest of Canaan as much as I do now. But even then I didn't like them, and I doubt that I read them more than once or twice. But the prophetic books and the psalms, especially the prophetic books, were and still are an inexhaustible source of vitality for me.

SCHULTZ: Wouldn't you like to publish them with your own commentary someday?

FROMM: I've already published a book of that kind, *You Will Be Like God,* an interpretation of the Jewish tradition. In it I tried to interpret the psalms, to distinguish between those that reflect some inner movement, a shift from sadness to joy, and those quite different ones that maintain the same mood and that are in a certain sense, though not always, somewhat self-righteous. At the very least there is no inner conflict in them, no inner movement. There are psalms that can be understood only if we notice that the speaker begins in a state of despair. Then he overcomes his despair, but it comes back. And he overcomes it again. And only when he has hit rock bottom, when his despair is most intense, does a sudden, miraculous change come about, a change accompanied by a jubilant, religious, hopeful mood. Psalm 22, which begins with the words, "My God, my God, why hast thou foresaken me?" is a good example.

An interesting point I might mention here is that people have often wondered why Jesus spoke these words of despair at his death. That question puzzled me when I was still a child. His words do not seem in keeping with his voluntary death and with his faith. But there really is no contradiction here because, as I have shown in detail in my book, the psalms are cited differently in the Jewish tradition and in the Christian. Where the Christian tradition cites a psalm by number, the Jewish tradition evokes the entire psalm by quoting the first sentence or the first few words. So what the Bible is telling us in this passage is that Jesus recited all of Psalm 22. And if you read this psalm, you will see that it begins in despair but ends as a hymn of hope. Perhaps more than any other psalm it expresses the universalistic, messianic message of early Christianity. We overlook this if we fail to see the shift that takes place in that psalm and if we think Jesus spoke only the first sentence of it. This sentence was even changed in the Gospel later because it caused misunderstandings. Well, we're getting a bit far afield here. But then it's nice that we're not bound by a program or schedule.

So that is one of the major influences in my life, and when I read the prophets today they are as fresh and alive for me as they were fifty years ago, perhaps even fresher and more alive.

The second great influence, Karl Marx, came later. What drew me to him was primarily his philosophy and his vision of socialism, which expressed, in secular form, the idea of human self-realization, of total humanization, the idea of a human being whose goal is vital self-expression and not the acquisition and accumulation of dead, material things. This theme is first struck in Marx's philosophical writings of 1844. If you read those writings without knowing who wrote them and if you do not know your Marx very well, then it's highly unlikely you'll guess Marx as the author. Those texts are not atypical for Marx, but it is difficult for us to see him in them because the Stalinists on the one hand and most socialists on the other have falsified our image of Marx so drastically, as if all that concerned him was economic change. The fact is that he saw economic change only as a means to an end. What really counted for Marx was the liberation of man in a humanistic sense. If you compare Goethe's and Marx's philosophies you'll find some astonishing similarities. Marx is firmly rooted in the humanistic tradition and, I think, in the prophetic one as well. And if you read one of the boldest and most radical of thinkers, Meister Eckhart, you will no doubt be surprised to find many similarities with Marx in him, too.

SCHULTZ: It's true that we have to defend Marx—and many of his colleagues of the most varied schools—from his own disciples. But who is doing this defending? And the same question can be extended to include Brecht or Freud or Ernst Bloch or just about any creative spirit whose name people invoke for their own purposes today. Where in our universities or anywhere else are attempts being made to save authors like Marx from ossified, one-sided interpretation?

FROMM: There are very few Marx specialists today who do not see him totally in the light of rightest or leftist distortions. They use him to shore up their own views but not only their own views. They also use him to justify practices and policies that are often diametrically opposed to what Marx thought and wanted. When state capitalists of the Russian stamp or Western capitalists of the liberal stamp—and here I have the majority of Social Democratic ideologues in mind—when such people turn to Marx as their authority, they falsify Marx. The number of people who understand Marx today, really understand him, is very small. That may sound arrogant if I say that just about everybody is wrong except for me and a few others. I don't mean to be so sweeping in my judgment, but I do feel most Marx experts overlook the fact that Marx's thought is essentially religious, though not "religious" in the sense that it posits any faith in God. Buddhism isn't religious in that sense either. Buddhism does not recognize a god, but it is religious in its central belief that we have to transcend our narcissism, our egoism, our inner isolation, and open ourselves to life, that we—as Meister Eckhart would put it—have to make ourselves empty so that we can be made full, so that we can become whole. That belief, expressed in different words, is at the heart of Marx's work. I've often had a little fun reading selections from Marx's economic-philosophical manuscripts to various people. I recall a meeting I had with Dr. Suzuki, an eminent figure in Zen Buddhism. I read him some passages without telling him who had written them, and then I asked him: Is that Zen? Yes, of course, he said. That's Zen. Another time I read some similar passages to a group of very learned theologians, and their guesses ranged from all kinds of classical authors, such as Thomas Aquinas, to the most modern theologians. Not one of them suspected that the author was Marx. They simply didn't know Marx.

There are a number of Marx scholars, such as Ernst Bloch, for example, who see that side of Marx clearly; and anti-Marxist Catholic scholars like Jean Ives Calvez see it, too. Their number is not all that small, but their influence, compared to that of the dominant schools of Marx interpretation, has remained small, except among theologians.

Another key influence for me was Johann Jakob Bachofen, an author who is, unfortunately, not very well known any more. Bachofen was the first thinker to discover matriarchal society. He wrote his major work about 110 years ago. The first translation of it into English—and not a complete translation at that—appeared only five years ago. Bachofen discovered that a matriarchal world had existed before the patriarchal one. He did not just state that as a general proposition, but he also showed what the difference was between the matriarchal and patriarchal positions. The matriarchal position—to state the case briefly—stands for the principle of unconditional human love. A mother loves her children without any regard for their merits. She loves them because they are her children. And if a mother loved her baby only when it smiled sweetly and was well behaved, then many a child would starve to death. A father loves his children because they obey him, because they are like him. Now I am not speaking here about every mother or every father but rather about types or categories, about the classic types we see exemplified throughout the history of paternal and maternal love. Taken individually, people are so mixed that we find many maternal fathers and many paternal mothers. The difference has to do with the social order, with whether it is patriarchal or matriarchal. The conflict between the two is nowhere more beautifully articulated than in Sophocles' *Antigone*. Antigone embodies the matriarchal principle: "I am here not to hate but to love," while Creon embodies the patriarchal one, the principle that makes the state supreme over all other human values (and a principle that we would call fascist today).

Bachofen's discovery gave me a key not only for understanding history, not only for understanding so many things in our patriarchal society in which love is made dependent on performance, but also for understanding what I have come to see more and more as the central problem in individual human development: What meaning—in women as well as in men—does our longing for a mother have? What constitutes the bond to the mother? What does it really mean? What is the nature of the Oedipus complex? Is it a sexual bond? I don't think so. It has to do with the most profound bond human beings can experience, a longing for some extraordinary figure, a goddess, who relieves us of our responsibilities, eliminates the risks of life, indeed, even relieves us of our fear of death, and shelters us in a kind of paradise. For that protection, we pay the price of dependence on the mother, the price of not fully becoming ourselves. These are all important problems, and so Bachofen became extremely important for me in the early 1920s.

Another major influence was Buddhism. It made me realize that there was such a thing as a religious position that could manage without God. I first encountered Buddhism about 1926, and it was one of the greatest experiences of my life. My interest in Buddhism has never faded, and later study of Zen Buddhism, especially with Dr. Suzuki but also through a great deal of reading, has only deepened that interest.

And of course I haven't mentioned Sigmund Freud yet. I got to know Freud's work at this same time, and it too has remained central to my thinking. These influences, then—prophetic Judaism, Marx, matriarchy, Buddhism, and Freud—were the key ones that formed not only my thinking but my entire development, for I have never had, and have never been able to acquire to this very day, the ability to think about things I cannot make come alive in my imagination. I have no gift for abstract thought. I can think only those thoughts that relate to something I can concretely experience. If that relationship is lacking, my interest fades, and I can't mobilize my abilities.

SCHULTZ: Despite the fact that you know Marx quite well—or I should say *because* you know Marx quite well—you are not exactly what anyone would call a typical Marxist, and I have the sense that your relationship with Freud is similar. You take Freud—as we are fond of saying these days—as a point of departure. And if we take that phrase at face value, it means that you depart from him and part with him. You go beyond him. And in that respect you are unlike the great majority of Freudians, of whom— if I see the situation correctly—you are quite critical.

FROMM: I've always been in the minority. With Bachofen I've been in the minority because Bachofen's following is quite small and can't help being a minority. As for Freud, I was trained as a strict Freudian in the Berlin Institute, and at first I totally accepted Freud's theories on sexuality and so forth. I was, in that respect, always a good student who assumed initially that his teachers were right until his own experience proved differently. I didn't begin to protest until I knew something myself. That does not seem to be the way protestors operate today, but it was the way they did then, and that was the route I took. Anyhow, I studied Freud very thoroughly, and there was, of course, great pressure on us to accept Freudian theory. But then after a few years I began to have my doubts. I began to realize more and more that I was not really finding what I was supposed to find in my patients' material but was interpreting Freudian theory into their material. And I realized something else as well: Freudian theory was simply not enabling me to reach the patient and his real problems. I do not want to go into Freudian theory here. That is a complex business. But as a Freudian I had been trained to see everything in terms of the Oedipus complex, of fear of castration, of sexuality in general, and of the fears related to it.

I frequently found that this theory was not relevant to the patients I was dealing with. And something else happened that I found extremely unpleasant: I became bored. I sat there and did everything the way I had been taught to do it. I didn't go so far as to fall asleep. (One of my teachers did, and he claimed it wasn't such a bad thing. When he went to sleep during an analysis, he said, he sometimes had a dream that gave him more insight into the case than he could have gained by listening to the patient. But that was pure rationalization, of course.) I realized that I was becoming tired and that I was completely worn out after six, seven, or eight hours. And I asked myself: Why is it that you're so tired? Why are you so bored? With time I came to see that my boredom stemmed from the fact that I was not in touch with the life of my patients, that I was dealing in abstractions, even though those

106

abstractions went in the guise of primitive experiences that had supposedly occurred in a patient's childhood.

But as I began to shift my attention more and more to what struck me as truly central to my work, that is, to the relationship of one human being to another and to the specifically human emotions that are rooted not in instinct but rather in man's existence as a human being, then I began to see, then I began truly to understand; and the person I was analyzing could understand what it was I was saying, too. He felt: Aha, so that's the way it is. I didn't feel tired any more, and my sessions with patients were very lively. I often thought that even if analysis brought the patient no relief from his symptoms—and that is, unfortunately, sometimes the case—then the hours he spent in analysis would still remain among the most stimulating, enlivening hours of his life; for during those hours he came alive. And then if I found myself becoming tired despite this, I would say to my patient: "Look, what's going on here? I didn't feel this tired when you came, and now I'm feeling exhausted. Is that coming from something you've said? Or what have I done to make things so dreary here?" And so I came to judge the success or failure of a session by whether it had been interesting or not, no matter what else happened in it. And interest was generated not by clever or brilliant formulations but by having both partners address what was relevant, what was of genuine concern to them.

SCHULTZ: The influences you have named for us here—the prophets, Marx, Bachofen, Freud, and Buddhism—clearly stand in some relationship to each other but are also so disparate that it seems remarkable indeed that you have been able to draw them together into a kind of mosaic or—as a few of your friends have put it—into a creative synthesis. Do you feel this synthesizing impulse is characteristic for your work?

FROMM: Yes, I think so. My deepest intellectual and emotional impulse has been to break down the walls between these apparently disparate elements, all of which, by the way, with the exception of Buddhism, are basic building blocks in the formation of European culture. I wanted to find the shared structure in them and, if you will, bring them together in a synthesis. Actually, though, it is incorrect to speak of a synthesis here, for what I wanted to show was that these different schools of thought are only different facets of one basic attitude, one basic concept. Perhaps I can best explain what I mean here simply by saying that Meister Eckhart and Marx are my two favorite authors. Now most people will probably think that Marx and Eckhart are impossible bedfellows and that I must be rather daft if I think they belong together. But Eckhart's radicalism and Marx's philosophy are profoundly similar in their ability to probe down through the surface and to the root of things. As Eckhart says: The root of a thing explains its growth. Marx could have said that. So could Freud. We are in the habit of categorizing authors and their works. We emphasize one aspect of a writer; we see this or that about him but not the essence, not the whole. What I wanted to do was to see in context and to bring together in a vital way important elements that are basic to European thought but are usually regarded as separate from each other. That impulse has been at the heart of everything I have tried to do over the past forty years.

SCHULTZ: Now, if it is all right with you, I would like to break off our conversation momentarily and allow both you and our listeners a small artistic interlude. I know, Professor Fromm, that you enjoy listening to music and that you like to share this pleasure with your guests. Unlike your Frankfurt colleague, Theodor W. Adorno, you do not consider yourself an expert on music, but you are a great enthusiast of it. What are your likes and dislikes in the way of music?

FROMM: My musical taste is very old-fashioned. I do not bring any expertise to music, but it is immensely important to me on an experiential level. It is hard for me to imagine living anywhere where I would not be able to listen to music.

SCHULTZ: In looking at your records I found a lot of baroque music and Mozart, especially concertos for violin and woodwinds, and a lot of Beethoven. But you told me that if there is any music that would top your list of favorites it would be Bach's suites for cello as performed by Pablo Casals. Casals, who came upon these suites as a boy and who practiced them for twelve years before he could work up the courage to play them in public, has called them the "quintessence of Bach's work." I've brought along these six suites tonight, and we will spend a few minutes listening to them. But before we do, I'd like to make a brief remark by way of introduction. I recently saw a television interview with Casals that was made a few years before his death. At one point the interviewer asked Casals what he would say if he were suddenly given a chance to speak to the entire world. "I would tell people this," he said: "Deep in your hearts almost all of you want more peace than war, more life than death, more light than darkness. And then," he went on, "to make clear to them what I mean, which is not sentimental harmony but powerful vitality, I would play Bach for them."

SCHULTZ: Professor Fromm, you have just invested five to six years of work in a book called *The Anatomy of Human Destructiveness*. We might describe it as a debunking book, because its purpose is to debunk a great many very widespread ideas about human aggression. In one chapter that is of particular interest to German readers you attempt a characterization of Hitler. Here, too, your purpose appears to be to debunk, for what you have written is fundamentally different from the rest of the current literature on Hitler.

FROMM: There have been a few recent publications, written by former Nazis, that praise Hitler to the skies, but they probably will not draw any great readership. The two major books that have appeared in Germany are by Fest and Maser. A book by Langer was published in America. That book has a strange history. It was commissioned by the OSS during World War II so that the American intelligence services would have a psychological portrait of Hitler. The author is a psychoanalyst of the most orthodox school. Like so many other documents that are kept secret in America even though there is nothing secret at all about their contents, that book too was kept secret until recently. The author did not, of course, have much material to go on, and he analyzed Hitler from a Freudian point of view. Hitler had an Oedipus complex; he witnessed his parents in sexual intercourse; and so on and so forth. And that is somehow supposed to explain Hitler. The approach is rather naive, because you cannot very well take data that may be helpful in explaining most people's characters and hope to explain as complex a character as Hitler's with it.

A French writer, Jacques Brosse, has given us a much better

analysis of Hitler, and when he manages to steer clear of the jargon of psychoanalysis, Brosse presents a very solid picture of Hitler's character. But when he does bog down in his own jargon, he develops ideas that are so abstruse, complex, and comical that it would take too much time even to mention them here. But for all that, when he puts aside his theoretical, analytical formulations and brings his insight and common sense to bear on his subject, his book is far and away the best of its kind.

My own analysis differs both from the historical studies that have recently appeared in Germany and from the attempts to write psychological biographies of Hitler. In *Escape from Freedom,* published in 1941, I attempted a brief analysis of Hitler that did not, however, go into his childhood. My latest effort, which is longer and makes use of all the historical material currently available, is much more ambitious. In my first study, I saw Hitler primarily as a sadomasochist, that is (in my definition), a person with an unlimited passion for exerting power and control over others but also for subjugation of the self. Now, in the light of more extensive study and better insight, I have come to consider another factor even more important. I call this factor necrophilia. Ordinarily that term is applied only to a sexual perversion, but in using it as I do, I am following the example of the great Spanish philosopher Unamuno, who said in a speech he gave in Salamanaca in 1936 that the Falangist motto "Long live death" was a necrophilic motto. What I mean by necrophilia in a nonsexual and nonphysical sense is a fascination with everything that is dead, lifeless, with everything having to do with dismemberment, with the destruction of living relationships. The necrophiliac is motivated not by a love for the living but by an attraction to the purely mechanical. Necrophilia means love for what is dead. *Nekros* means corpse. Necrophilia is not a love of *death* but a love of *dead things,* of everything that is not alive. Its opposite is love of the living, a love for everything that grows, that has structure, that forms a unity, that is not dismembered.

But to come back to Hitler: If we are to be altogether honest, we have to admit that the simple fact that Hitler initiated a war that brought death to millions of people is not something for which he alone can be censured. Generals and statesmen have been doing that for the last 6,000 years, usually with the rationalization that they had to do it for the fatherland, and so on. What separates Hitler from many generals and statesmen who have wanted war is that he killed defenseless people. But the main intent of my analysis of Hitler is to show that Hitler was a man who felt a profound hatred for everything alive. If we say that Hitler hated the Jews, that is of course correct; but then it is not correct either, because it is much too limited a statement. He hated the Jews, but he also hated the Germans. For when victory slipped out of his hands and he saw he could not realize his ambition, he wanted all of Germany to go down with him. He had even expressed that wish as early as 1942. He said that if Germany lost the war, then the German people did not deserve to live. Hitler is an extreme example of a necrophiliac whose assurances that he would change everything for the better hid his real character from his followers.

Hitler had a facial expression that is characteristic for many necrophiliacs. They look as if they smell something rotten, but there is no bad odor present. What this indicates is that these people regard living things, not dead ones, as filth, and they consequently relate to them in this archaic way—by smelling and sniffing. Von Hentig cited a great many cases of that kind from criminological literature, individuals who enjoy smelling foul odors, for example. That is very characteristic for such types. They are attracted to bad smells or to excrement and carrion. This perversion is visible in their facial expressions. With necrophilic types you will find that the face remains immobile. They do not react; they are frozen. With biophilic people, the face shows a great variety of expressions, and it lights up in the presence of whatever is alive.

Another way we can express this is to say that the necrophiliac is hopelessly boring. A biophile is never boring. It doesn't matter what he talks about. The subject can be quite insignificant, but whatever he says is always marked by vitality. A necrophiliac may say something intelligent, but it does not come alive. We've all had the experience of hearing an intellectual say something terribly clever, yet we are bored by it. Conversely, a much less brilliant person can say something quite simple (this is bringing us back to our starting point this evening, the subject of conversation), and we are not bored at all. On the contrary, we are stimulated, because it is life that is speaking to us. We are always drawn to what is alive. It is vitality that makes people attractive. These days people seem to think—we men talk this way, and the cosmetic industry tries to convince women that it is true—we seem to think people can make themselves attractive and lovable if they paint their faces this way or that way or adopt a certain expression that is supposed to be modern and irresistible. A lot of people fall for that kind of thing, usually people who don't have much of a self. There is only one thing that really attracts us, and that is vitality. We can observe that in people who are falling in love. In their desire to please and attract the other, they in fact become livelier than they usually are. The only problem with this is that once they have achieved their goal and "have" each other, their desire to be more alive is much reduced. Then they suddenly become quite different, and after a while they don't love each other any more. They don't even know why they fell in love in the first place. Their partners are changed. They are no longer beautiful, because they no longer have the beauty that vitality brings to the face.

A necrophiliac's face is never beautiful, because it is never alive. You can see that in pictures of Hitler. He couldn't laugh freely and spontaneously. Speer told me how excruciatingly boring the noon and evening meals were with Hitler. He talked and talked and never noticed how bored everyone was. And he was so bored himself that he sometimes fell asleep while he was talking. That lack of vitality is typical for the necrophiliac.

I developed the concepts of necrophilia and biophilia on the basis of my clinical experience, but Freud's concepts of eros and the death wish contributed to my thinking, too. I originally rejected the idea of a "death wish," as did most analysts, because it seemed to me a product of pure speculation with no basis in fact. But then my own clinical experience made me realize that though Freud's theoretical concept was open to question Freud had, as he had done so often before, put his finger on something of tremendous importance, namely, that the two basic tendencies in people are a *propensity for life* and a *propensity for death and destruction*. Freud characterized those two tendencies very succinctly. He said that eros, the vital force or the force of love, strives for the integration of the whole, for union, while the goal of the death wish is disintegration or, as I would call it, dismemberment, dissection.

There are two points in which Freud's concepts and my own terms of necrophilia and biophilia differ. First, in Freud the two forces are equal in strength. The desire to destroy, he says, is as strong in people as is their joy in life. I don't think that is so. The evidence of biology does not support Freud here, for if we assume that the preservation of life is the supreme biological law, then from the standpoint of survival of the species it makes no sense that self-destructive tendencies are as powerful as the impulse to preserve and enhance life. There is still another point I would like to cite against Freud's view: We can demonstrate that destructive tendencies, that is, tendencies growing out of the death wish, result from failures in the art of living. They are the consequences of not living correctly.

We can show that people who have no chance to be free and to develop their own powers, people who are hemmed in, who live in a class or in a society in which everything functions in a mechanical, lifeless way—these people lose their capacity for spontaneity. The petty bourgeoisie, the class from which Hitler's most devoted followers came—these were people whose economic and social possibilities were next to nil, people who were without hope because the growth of modern capitalism had doomed their class to economic decline. And when the Nazis painted those people an idyllic picture in which the department stores would belong to all the little shopkeepers and everyone would have his niche, the picture was demagogically very powerful despite the fact that it was totally unrealistic. National Socialism did not, after all, do anything to slow the growth of capitalism; on the contrary, it let capitalism develop unchecked.

This link between thwarted vitality and necrophilia is evident in individuals, too. It is by no means rare to find people whose families were so "dead" that the children never experienced even the faintest breath of life during their childhoods. Everything was bureaucratized, routined, subject to rules. Life consisted solely of possessing things, owning things. The parents regarded any sign of spontaneity in their children as inherently bad. It is clear beyond any doubt that children are naturally very lively and active, a fact proved by recent neurophysiological and psychological studies. The child becomes more and more discouraged and then takes another direction, a direction in which the nonliving becomes central. In the final analysis we can say that a person who finds no joy in living will try to avenge himself and will prefer to destroy life rather than feel that he can make no sense of his life at all. He may still be alive physiologically, but psychologically he is dead. That is what gives rise to the active desire to destroy and to the passionate need to destroy everyone, including oneself, rather than confess that one has been born yet has failed to become a living human being. That is a bitter feeling for those who experience it, and we are not indulging in mere speculation if we assume that the wish to destroy follows on this feeling as an almost inevitable reaction.

SCHULTZ: Do you think that such necrophilia is on the increase?

FROMM: Yes, I'm afraid it is. I'm afraid that our preoccupation with everything mechanical encourages it. We are running away from life. It is difficult to explain in any concise way why it is that *things* are taking the place of *human beings* in our cybernetic society and culture, pushing human beings aside. As we mentioned earlier this evening, people are becoming increasingly *uncertain about their own being.* When I speak of "being" here I am using a term of great importance in the history of philosophy. What is being? I am less interested in its philosophical meaning here than I am in its experiential aspect. Let me give a simple example. A woman might come to an analyst and begin describing herself something like this: Well, Doctor, I "have" a problem. I "have" a happy marriage, and I "have" two children, too, but I'm "having" so many difficulties. Every sentence she produces uses the verb "to have." The entire world is represented as an object of having. In earlier times (and I know this from my own experience in both English and German) she would have said: I *feel* miserable, I *am* satisfied, I *am* worried, I *love* my husband or perhaps I *do not love* him or I *doubt* that I love him. In language like that, people speak about what they are, about their own activity, about the feelings they experience, not about objects or possessions. People are more and more inclined to express their being with nouns followed by some form of the verb "to have." I *have* everything, but I *am* nothing.

SCHULTZ: If someone can pronounce and elucidate the word "life" with as much power as you do, and if, in your view, people can no longer achieve a humane future in the name of the nation or of the law or of the party or of necessity or of God or of any other authorities we might come up with, if they can achieve such a future only *in the name of life,* then your interest in life must lead to an interest in the *conditions* in which life can flourish, a society that does not yet exist. Can you imagine conditions that would be favorable to life? Does your concept of biophilia have political consequences? Unlike most of your psychoanalytical colleagues you are a political creature through and through (and a very independent one at that). Being politically active is not, in your case, synonymous with party politics. Perhaps one is in a better position to take partisan stands when one is not bound by party affiliation. That is all clearly related to your theoretical position. Could you perhaps comment somewhat further on this?

FROMM: I'd be glad to, for you have touched on an important issue for all of us both personally and as a society. You're quite right. During the years in which most people are inclined to join a political party, that is, in their youth, I never belonged to one. I was a member of the American Socialist Party for a few years, but, in my view, it swung so far to the right that even if I viewed its possibilities with the greatest optimism, I could no longer remain a member of it. I am an extremely political person, but neither in politics nor anywhere else can I cling to illusions simply because they support my "line." Lies can tie us to a party, but ultimately it is only the truth that can lead to the liberation of man. But too many people are afraid of freedom and prefer illusions to it.

SCHULTZ: Because they take a party line. Party politics can put blinders on us. We could say, in a certain sense, that party politics can make us apolitical. I don't mean that as an attack on political parties, nor do I deny their necessity, but I do feel that when our political life is dominated by party politics, we run the danger of becoming unpolitical.

FROMM: Yes, parties, especially the most progressive ones, which, by the way, hardly exist any more as parties, would need much more independent people. It is essential to our political lives that there be politically active people who, from their own perspectives, come right out and say what they think, what they know. Private and public life cannot be separated. We cannot split off our knowledge of ourselves from our knowledge of society. Both belong together. This is, I think, an error committed by Freud and many analysts who felt that the two things could be separated, that we could gain complete understanding of ourselves but remain blind to social processes. That just isn't so, if for no other reason than that truth is indivisible. We cannot see reality here and remain closed to it there. That dulls our cutting edge and makes our search for the truth ineffectual. And we can see ourselves rightly only if we can see others rightly, only if we can see them in the context of their social circumstances, which is to say, only if we look sharply and critically at all that is going on around us in the world. This is what love demands of us, too. And if we love our fellow humans, we cannot limit our insight and our love only to others as individuals. That will inevitably lead to mistakes. We have to be political people, I would even say passionately involved political people, each of us in the way that best suits our own temperaments, our working lives, and our own capabilities.

I'd like to add one other thing that belongs in this context. The intellectual has one prime task to fulfill, first, last, and always. It is his job to search out the truth as best he can and to speak that truth. It is not the intellectual's primary calling, it is not his primary function, to draft political platforms. And to say this does not contradict what I have just been saying about political activity. But it is the intellectual's special task—and this is what defines his role or should define it—to pursue the truth without compromise and without regard for his own or anyone else's interests. If intellectuals restrict their function of finding and speaking the whole truth in the service of any party program or any political goals, no matter how praiseworthy the program or the goals may be, then those intellectuals are failing in their own unique task and, ultimately, in the most important *political* task they have. For I feel that political progress depends on how much of the truth we know, how clearly and boldly we speak it, and how great an impression it makes on other people.

Hitler—Who Was He and What Constituted Resistance Against Him?

SCHULTZ: The question of political resistance is receiving more and more attention everywhere in the world. There are many causes for resistance, and there are many forms it takes. Under certain circumstances we have a right to resist, even a duty to resist.

Gandhi developed a wide range of theoretical possibilities and strategic escalations, which he then put into practice with remarkable success. But it is eminently clear in his case that resistance did not consist only in applying certain methods for maximum effect; it consisted, too, in an attitude based on conviction and involving the whole man in every aspect of his existence. Gandhi compared practitioners of nonviolent resistance with soldiers. They have to be ready to lay down their lives. But their courage is not a courage for war; it is a courage for peace. Their great weapon is their refusal to use weapons. Only now are we beginning to grasp the great political significance of his theory of nonviolent resistance. Hitler was not faced with anything comparable to the timely and carefully planned resistance Gandhi turned against British colonial power.

But resistance against Hitler is the question here, the resistance that did take shape against him and the resistance that did not.

But if we are to understand what resistance against him meant we first have to know who this man was. How could political power as irrationally based as his was ever grow to such proportions?

If we look into the wealth of literature now available about Hitler, we will be struck by how little curiosity most authors show about him. Their explanations of his personality are for the most part rather pat, and a good number of writers conclude that if the resistance against Hitler had been more effectively organized it could have succeeded.

Is that true? Did the men and women of the resistance achieve sufficient clarity on whom or what it was they were resisting? Was adequate opposition possible at all as long as the intellectual tools at hand were inadequate for grasping the complexity of Hitler's personality and political impact? Many members of the resistance understood quite clearly just who and what Hitler was. But they had to deal not just with a single individual but with a *mass phenomenon*. They found themselves playing a losing game. They did not feel they had the support of large segments of the population who had also seen the light. (To what extent they even wanted democratic backing is another whole question we will not take time to look into here.) They lived with the unsettling feeling that they were acting both too early and too late. Hitler's fall was long overdue, but was the population mature enough to function politically without Hitler? That doubt played a major and controlling role in the thinking of many key leaders in the conspiracy.

Professor Fromm, unlike many of your colleagues you began agitating early in your career for a new political psychology and anthropology. The perspective that you have brought to the assessment of Hitler seems to me essential, because it enlarges on other points of view at the same time that it calls them into question.

FROMM: Who was this man Hitler? The question of who someone is or was will hold varying degrees of interest for us depending on the personality involved, but it is an appropriate question to ask about anyone. Who is he? Who am I? Are there any final answers to those questions? This inquiry is as difficult with Hitler as it would be for anyone else, for every individual is a tangle of motives, impulses, and contradictions. Along with everything that a person consciously understands about himself there are all those things he feels and does unconsciously, and so we never come to a complete answer to the question: Who was, who is this person? Who am I? But it would be wrong to use that insight as an excuse for retreating into relativism and saying that we simply can't know at all who others are or who we are. We can in fact know quite a lot, enough to serve us for all practical purposes, enough to know whether someone will be a blessing or a curse on our lives. With these reservations in mind, I'd like to venture some remarks about this man Hitler.

If we look at his biography, we can probably safely say that from his childhood on he lived in a fantasy world. He had delusions of grandeur that relieved him, and indeed prevented him, from adapting himself to reality. In *Mein Kampf* he claimed that he had come into conflict with his father because he wanted to be an artist and his father had wanted him to become a civil servant. But that was not the real conflict.

For Hitler, and for a number of other people as well, being an artist meant being free of all obligations and free to pursue nothing but one's own fantasies. It does not seem to have been so crucial to Hitler's father that Hitler become a civil servant, though that was a natural choice for the father to make, because he was a civil servant himself. What the father came to understand more and more was that his son had no sense of responsibility or discipline and that he was doing nothing to find an active role in life or to direct his life toward some goal. And so Hitler, like many narcissistic individuals, experienced one disappointment after another. As his delusions of grandeur became more inflated, the abyss between them and his actual accomplishments yawned all the wider. And from that abyss arose resentment, anger, hatred, and ever greater delusions; for the less Hitler achieved in reality, the more he gave himself over to fantasy. It was evident from his earliest years. Hitler went to Vienna, failed his exams at art school, and then decided to try architecture. But to qualify for admission to the study of architecture he would have had to take another year of school. He was unable to do that and didn't want to. Instead, he kept it a secret from everyone, including his best friend, that he had failed in his art school exam, and he wandered about in the streets of Vienna sketching the façades of imposing buildings. He thought that was the way to become an architect.

He finally wound up as a small businessman, a commercial artist, if you will. He made extremely pedantic copies of original drawings and paintings and never, or hardly ever, worked from nature. He sold those copies and earned a small, modest income.

Measured against his grand ideas of himself, Hitler was a total failure, until the war came along. In the war he "woke up." Now he could identify with Germany and did not have to produce anything independently any more. And he was in fact a brave and reliable soldier. But his officers soon came to complain about his obsequiousness toward his superiors. That was a deeply rooted characteristic in him that would never disappear, even later when he was in power himself and was in a position to make everyone else lick his boots. There was no one above him then, except for "fate" and "the laws of nature" and "Providence," to which he did bow.

That is one side of Hitler's personality. Another was his extreme narcissism. What is narcissism? It is something we can all observe. It is easy to see in others, somewhat harder to see in ourselves. A narcissistic person considers only those things real and important that directly affect him. My ideas, my body, my possessions, my opinion, my feelings—all those things are real. And what is not mine is pale stuff that hardly exists at all. In pathological cases, narcissism can be so extreme that an individual is incapable of even perceiving what is going on in the outside world. Hitler remained narcissistic his whole life. He was never interested in anything but himself. Where his mother or his friends were concerned, he was disinterested, almost without feeling. Indeed, he had no friends; he lived completely isolated from others; he cared only about himself, his plans, his power, his will.

Perhaps Hitler's most important character trait was *necrophilia.* That is love for what is dead, for destruction, for everything that is not alive. Necrophilia is a complicated subject, and I can't go into it in great detail here. But perhaps I can adequately suggest what it involves. There are people we can characterize by saying that they love life. And there are others of whom we can say that they hate life. People who love life are easy to recognize. And there is nothing more attractive than this kind of loving person in whom we see that he loves not just something or someone but that he loves *life.* But there are people who do not love life, who are more inclined to hate life, who are drawn to the inanimate and, ultimately, to death.

SCHULTZ: But then how was it possible that Hitler's necrophilic influence didn't evoke more resistance than it did, more antipathy, more revulsion? Doesn't that lack of negative response suggest that necrophilia was widespread in the population, at least in some latent form? There must have been some kind of link, some mutual tie, even cooperation, between Hitler and those who followed him, agreed with him, and obeyed him.

FROMM: The answer to that question is a complex one. First of all, there was indeed a great resemblance between Hitler's character and that of his fanatical followers. If we look at this group from the standpoint of sociology and social psychology, we find that the most zealous National Socialists came from the petit-bourgeoisie, that is, from a class that was without hope, full of resentment, and itself sadomasochistic in character. The type has been jokingly described as the "bicyclist's character," because such individuals bow from the waist to those above them and kick with their feet at those below them. Those people found nothing worthy of love or interest left in their lives, so they turned their energies to acquiring power over others and even to self-destruction.

The next point I want to make is that Hitler was an actor. He was such a superb actor that he could make people believe his goals were the salvation, the wellbeing of Germany. He did that so skillfully that millions of people believed him and simply ignored the truth. Hitler had an incredible talent for turning human gullibility to his advantage. Call it charisma, hypnosis, demagogy, or what you will, he seems to have exerted a power over people that made them eager to submit to him (many reports mention people succumbing to his glance). The mechanism worked something like this: First people would submit to him, then they would believe whatever he said. He once said himself that meetings should be held in the evening when people are tired. That makes them more gullible, and they will offer less intellectual resistance to what they are told. All those factors working together allowed Hitler to recruit loyal followers whom he deceived because he hid his destructiveness from them. There were millions who did not understand what his real goals were. They ran after him like rats after the pied piper without realizing where he was leading them.

SCHULTZ: He was, on the one hand, a seducer. He was somebody who came "from above." He was also what we call a "strong man" who promised not just solutions but also salvation. On the other hand, though, it seems to me he came "from below," or at least his rise was made possible from below. He was a product of expectations and circumstances. I have the sense that any strong man—seen in this way—is a weak man. He owes his strength to the constellation that makes him representative for many others. Strength that takes the form of resistance is of a completely different order. Hitler would probably never have been capable of resistance in the sense we mean here. Or am I seeing things wrongly? I'm intrigued by this strange relationship between the "leader" and those who are led or misled.

FROMM: I think you're absolutely right. Hitler was the kind of leader who needed the masses behind him to feel strong. He was not someone who could develop and propagate an idea without applause to help him along. He needed applause; he needed others' enthusiasm to feel confirmed in himself. His sense of power came from the reactions of the people he spoke to. That was clear from the outset, in the small, initial circle of twenty-one men who first constituted the National Socialist Workers' Party in Munich. Like all narcissists, he was so full of himself that every word he spoke seemed to him to contain the greatest wisdom and truth. But he needed others who believed in him before he could believe in himself. If no one besides himself had believed in him, he would have found himself on the edge of insanity, for his ideas did not derive from rationally based convictions. They were an expression of his emotional needs. They were based on his sense of his greatness and power, but, as we saw, he needed outside confirmation of that greatness and power. If we take away from him the applause and success, then what is left is a man on the verge of insanity. I don't mean to say that he was insane. He wasn't, but to state the case in extreme form, I would say that he protected himself from insanity by regarding his millions of followers as confirmation of his sanity and of the reality of his ideas. For him, it was applause that proved his ideas true, not the inner consistency of the ideas themselves. Hitler never showed any interest in what truth was. Like any other demagogue, he was interested only in what brought applause, for applause is what makes things true.

SCHULTZ: What you have been saying could provide valuable guidelines for the evaluation of any and all politicians and their policies.

But I fear that we are still a long way from the political maturity that would be immune to such invitations to irreality and immune to psychological subordination of this kind. But now, Professor Fromm, to come back to our original question, what would constitute resistance, mass disobedience, rebellion against the kind of man you have just been characterizing here?

FROMM: Let's take a look at this word "resistance" for a minute. To resist means to "take a stand against" something, and in order to do that we have to be somebody ourselves. Then we are not so easy to deceive or impress. On the contrary, we are capable of protest, rejection, outrage. But if we are to be able to do that we have to realize that when we're up against a "leader" like Hitler and his policies we are not dealing just with certain political views of what will best promote Germany's wellbeing but with components of character and emotion, indeed, with philosophical and religious components that run through those views.

Of course Hitler said he wanted what was best for Germany. Who wouldn't want that? But he did not say that one of his goals was the destruction and conquest of other countries. All he did was take defensive measures that would ensure that Germany could flourish. If we take that as a purely political statement, then all we can say is: All right, I think that is the right thing to do, or I think it is the wrong thing to do. I think the means are appropriate, or I think they are inappropriate. The issue remains one of rational calculation comparable to the calculations a businessman might make. But if we realize that all this is nothing but "rationalization" as defined by depth psychology and that these apparently rational arguments in no way reveal what is really at issue here, then we can see that Hitler's ideology is an expression and result of a necrophilic and sadomasochistic character of the type I have just described. We have to look *behind* the rational formulations and pay not so much attention to *what* a political leader says as to *how* he says it. We have to study his face, his gestures, the whole man. Only then can we see what kind of character this person has. Then we may see that this leader is a necrophiliac, someone whom we reject from the bottom of our hearts, someone who outrages us, someone we want nothing to do with, someone we can never befriend because all our powers are committed to the preservation of life and to the dignity of man, to his freedom. All the necrophiliac's powers are, by contrast, committed to destruction, to the subjugation of others, to putting them down, to dominating them. We have to stop just listening to words and start discovering who and what this man is who speaks such words. What is his nature, his character?

We should also note that in Hitler's case, as in so many others, we have to do not only with politics in a practical sense but also with philosophy, with religion, if you will. Everyone is religious in a broad sense of the word, which is to say he has goals that go beyond the mere necessities of earning a living; he has a vision and feelings that lead him to do more than be a machine for eating and reproducing. But today these impulses do not ordinarily take traditional religious forms any more but are often directed into the area of political and economic thinking and planning. The only problem is that we fail to see that we are still dealing with religious impulses. If we ask ourselves what Hitler's religion was, the answer would be a deification of the national ego, of domination, of inequality, of hatred. His was a pagan religion of power and destruction. It was more than just a pagan religion. It was the most extreme antithesis to the religion of Christianity or of Judaism or the humanistic tradition. Or to put this in somewhat different terms, we could say that in a certain sense Hitler's religion was one of social Darwinism. He held to the principle that what serves the improvement of the race is good. Man no longer acts on behalf of God, on behalf of justice, on behalf of love, but in the name of evolution. And there have been more than a few people since Darwin who have adopted social Darwinism as their new religion. The principles of evolution are the new gods, and Darwin is the new prophet. Perhaps the only thing Hitler truly believed in was that he was acting on behalf of, and carrying out, the laws of evolution, the laws of biology.

This kind of thinking is not limited to Hitler alone. It also crops up in Konrad Lorenz's writings on aggression. Lorenz's central philosophical idea is that we have to serve the laws of evolution. In 1941 Lorenz brought those ideas together in an essay in which he praised and agreed with a number of Hitler's laws concerning "racial hygiene," claiming that there was a basis in science for them.

Now, the question remains: Can we recognize the *philosophical, religious,* and *psychological factors* that really underlie the political formulations? Do we have the insight to see that the statements and protestations that claim to want nothing but the best are an expression of special psychic and philosophical types. Take what is perhaps the best known example, the French Revolution. *Liberté, egalité, fraternité*—those were the principles that motivated the people of that time, principles that may well be deeply rooted in human nature, in the nature of man's entire existence. Some neurophysiologists think those principles even have their origin in the structure of the human brain. Freedom is a necessity if the human organism is to function at its full capacity. Those ideas not only represented the political line of the French revolutionaries but were the product of Enlightenment philosophy as a whole, a philosophy that was deeply rooted in the hearts of a vast number of people. Historical circumstances had brought those people to the point where they became aware of those human demands and articulated them. In the same way Hitler's narcissism was a religion, too, though one with exactly the opposite aims; and that is why it attracted people of completely different character.

SCHULTZ: Perhaps we can illustrate that point in concrete terms by recalling Moltke and Freisler's encounter in the People's Court. The gist of what Moltke said in his closing statement was that National Socialism and Christianity did have something in common, but it was this same shared factor that also distinguished them from each other and made them enemies: They both demanded total commitment.

FROMM: Exactly. Moltke, in a situation of extreme danger, summarized in that one short sentence what I have been trying to say here with a lot of sentences. He went right to the heart of the matter and stated it with great precision.

SCHULTZ: Moltke made many remarkably clear and unconventional statements of that kind. His political thinking was very down-to-earth, and he had shown himself in any number of situations to be eminently practical, yet he still always regarded the *individual human being* as the focus of political interest. Moltke's ideas on public education were much influenced by Eugen Rosenstock-Huessy, who felt that the ultimate question in political education was *who* we *are*, not what our political views are or which party we belong to. That was not a popular view at the time, and it is no more popular today because it is misunderstood as a kind of privatism. But seen in the context of your interpretation it seems extremely pertinent. Resistance against Hitler, resistance that for the most part was never offered, would not have been mere verbal protest but rather life lived as an act of protest. But that kind of life as protest is not something that can be delegated to a few professional politicians. It is, so to speak, a layman's job, a job for everyone. Have social psychologists conducted any studies that might support this claim?

FROMM: Who is this person or that person? What is his character? This is a question not just of moral and psychological interest but also one of obvious political interest. Anyone who refuses to see that defines the limits of politics too narrowly. What was the characterological orientation of the majority of Germans? Did they represent a soil in which the seed Hitler sowed could flourish, or were they a dry soil inhospitable to that seed? In 1931 I joined some colleagues of mine at the Frankfurt Institute for Social Research in a study of this very question. Unfortunately, that study has never been published. [The study has since been published as *The Working Class in Weimar Germany* by Harvard University Press.]

The question we set ourselves was this: What are the chances for an effective resistance against Hitler if he should continue to gain power? How much resistance will the majority of the population offer him, particularly those people whose *opinions* run against him, that is, the workers and, to a large extent, the white-collar workers, too? We chose to examine that question by means of a characterological analysis that did not deal with Hitler himself at all but did, for the first time, undertake the task of defining the authoritarian character. The authoritarian character has a structural predeliction to submit, to subordinate itself, but it also has a need to dominate. Those two things always go together; the one compensates for the other. The truly democratic or revolutionary character is just the opposite and will refuse both to dominate and to be dominated. For the democratic character the equality and dignity of man are deeply felt imperatives, and such a character will be drawn only to what promotes human dignity and equality.

Our theoretical premise was that what a person thinks is relatively unimportant. It is usually a matter of sheer chance and will depend on what kind of slogans the person has heard, on which party either family tradition or social circumstances have motivated him to join, on which ideologies he has come in contact with. He thinks more or less the same things that others think, which is a sign of the human tendency to conform and to forfeit independence. What a person thinks, then, we called *opinion*. Opinion can be easily changed. Opinion remains the same only as long as circumstances remain the same. And if I may make an aside here, I would point out that that is the great disadvantage of all polls that determine nothing but opinion. It is beyond the scope of such polls to ask: What would your opinion be tomorrow if circumstances were completely different? But in politics that is what counts, and the question of primary importance is not what someone happens to think *at the moment*. What is important is how he lives and acts. And how he lives and acts will depend on his character. If we put our question this way, then we find we are in need of another concept that you mentioned before, too; and that is the concept of *conviction*. Conviction is an opinion that is rooted in a person's character and not just in his head. Conviction is a product of what he *is;* opinion is often based only on what he *hears.* And so we concluded that only those people whose *convictions* were at odds with the terroristic system, not those whose *opinions* ran against it, would offer resistance to it. In other words, only those people who themselves had nonauthoritarian characters would speak out and resist and not be duped.

SCHULTZ: The approach you took in your study surprises me, and it is hard to imagine that a similar approach would ever find a place among the primarily quantitative polling methods used today. But it is not just public opinion research that ignores the question of character; our so-called political education and information is not interested in anything but "opinion" either.

FROMM: That is, unfortunately, the great failing of most studies of political attitudes and of all our efforts at political education. No allowance is made for the characterological and, if you will, the philosophical and religious factor that is inevitably present in all political life. Another concept that has been stressed primarily by Marxism is that of politics as the expression of economic and class interests. Marxists will always stress that aspect of politics over the one oriented to ostensible goals, and I think on the whole they are correct to do so. But there is something lacking in the Marxist concept, too. We have to take not just economic and social motives into account but also whatever emotions, whatever inner possibilities, are released in people, however close their link to socioeconomic factors may be. In other words, people do not act solely out of economic interest but also out of inner needs, feelings, goals that are deeply rooted in the "human condition," in the givens of human existence. I think we have to become thoroughly familiar with both these factors—with the economic motives *and* with the specifically human ones—if we want to understand why people act one way or another politically. Both factors are integrated in "social character."

This area represents a vast gap in our knowledge, one that psychology as a discipline has not addressed. And political science is still stalled, by and large, in an obsolete, rationalistic stage of inquiry that seems to assume that the role emotions play in politics cannot be the subject of empirical inquiry.

But if I may come back to our study in Frankfurt, what we set out to do was determine the dominant characterological set of German workers and office workers. We sent out to 2,000 people a questionnaire containing a great many detailed questions. About 600 of those came back; that was quite a normal rate of return for such a questionnaire at that time. Our questions did not follow the multiple-choice format usually used in such surveys, that is, a question followed by "yes" or "no" or "agree strongly" or "agree somewhat" or "don't agree at all." The answers were written out individually either by an interviewer or by the person being questioned. Then we analyzed the answers the way a psychiatrist or psychoanalyst analyzes answers in a session. What is the *unconscious* significance of that answer as opposed to what the patient is *consciously* thinking? And we found that if we analyzed each answer this way, a few hundred answers would give us a picture not only of what a person's conscious thoughts were but also of his character, of what he loved, of what repulsed him, of what attracted him, of what he wanted to see encouraged, of what he condemned and wanted to see negated.

Take this question, for example: "Is physical punishment essential in childrearing?" One person said no; another said yes. Those answers alone didn't tell us much about an individual's character. But if someone said, "No, it isn't a good thing because it limits a child's freedom, and a child should learn not to be afraid," then we read that as characteristic of a nonauthoritarian person. If someone else said, "Yes, because a child has to learn to fear his parents and be obedient," we interpreted that as a sign of an authoritarian character. Now, you can't draw conclusions like that on the basis of a single question. But our questionnaires had several hundred questions on them, and we ourselves were surprised to find how consistent the patterns on each questionnaire were. After reading the answers to ten questions you could guess quite accurately what the rest would be like.

Our final results fell out something like this: About 10 percent of the people responding to the questionnaire had authoritarian characters. We assumed that they would become ardent Nazis shortly before or after Hitler seized power. Another 15 percent had anti-authoritarian characters, and our theoretical assumption was that they would never become Nazis. Whether they would have the courage to risk their lives or their freedom was another question, but they would always remain passionate opponents of Nazi policies and ideology. The great majority, 75 percent, had mixed characters, as is often the case in the bourgeoisie. They were neither strongly authoritarian nor strongly anti-authoritarian but showed some evidence of both tendencies. Our assumption about them was that these were the people who would be neither zealous Nazis nor resistance fighters, because their characters were not clearly enough defined in either direction. They would probably go along with the crowd with varying degrees of enthusiasm or distaste.

Although we have no detailed information that can tell us what percentage of German blue-collar and white-collar workers became Nazis and what percentage resisted Nazism, in their hearts at least if not outwardly, I suspect that a sizable number of knowledgeable people would think the figures established by our study reflected reality quite accurately. Only a relatively small number of German workers joined the resistance; an even smaller number became committed Nazis. The great majority did neither the one nor the other. And so the resistance remained ineffectual. The prediction we made on a theoretical basis was, of course, an important one for assessing political reality and Hitler's prospects for success. And we can do the same thing in any country and with any population if we ask what the people *feel* and what they are, not just what they *think*. Once we have grasped this difference between conviction and opinion, we can demonstrate its existence empirically and on the basis of a concrete socioanalytical study.

SCHULTZ: You mentioned that your study was not published after its completion. Why not?

FROMM: It wasn't published because the directors of the institute didn't want to make it available to the public. I have a few ideas on why they didn't, but it would lead us too far afield to discuss them here.

SCHULTZ: Fear and caution may well have been involved. That is, in retrospect, regrettable, because release of that study might have brought about a change in awareness.

FROMM: Absolutely. But the study remained under lock and key. Some reports on the history of the institute have claimed that this study was never made, but those claims are incorrect. It was made, and the documentation from it is still available.

SCHULTZ: Are any comparable studies being made now?

FROMM: I don't know of any. My colleague Michael Maccoby and I applied the same principles in a study we made in a small Mexican village [published in volume III of Erich Fromm's collected works under the title "Psychoanalytische Charakterologie in Theorie and Praxis: Der Gesellschafts-Charakter eines mexikanischen Dorfes," Stuttgart, 1981]. That study was concerned not only with "authoritarian" and "anti-authoritarian" character traits but with others as well. The same methodology has been used and has held up very well in studies that Michael Maccoby has done on the difference between necrophiliacs and biophiles in different social classes in America. But it has not been imitated and developed further anywhere else.

SCHULTZ: Professor Fromm, how can we become better judges of human character in the political realm? Most of our politicians will not be particularly eager to see improvement in this line, but it seems essential to me for the health of a democracy that we sharpen our perceptions of the people who appear on our political stage. Television allows us to take a close look at their faces, to observe their gestures, and to look behind what they say. We have to learn to recognize the real motives behind all the verbal asseverations we hear. How can we do this?

FROMM: That is a crucial question, especially in a democracy. How can we prevent a democracy from falling prey to demagogues?

People in a democracy are supposed to judge for themselves. But how can they judge if they go on only what a politician says? They do, of course, have something more to go on. Voters take in a great deal subliminally and form judgments about a candidate's honesty, mendacity, candidness, decency, or evasiveness. We know that is so in the United States, and it is no doubt so in Germany, too. But the requisite skills are not anywhere near highly enough developed.

There are many prerequisites necessary to the functioning of a democracy, and I will not attempt to go into them all here. But we can say that a democracy will be able to function properly only if people are able to see what a politician's dominant tendencies and emotions are, what the philosophical and quasi-religious character behind his political positions and opinions is. And that means that we have to *unlearn* something first. We have to unlearn the practice of stressing what a person says, and we have to learn to look at the whole person.

It is interesting how skillful we are at this when it comes to our business lives. If we are about to hire someone or enter into a partnership with him, we are not usually so stupid as to listen only to what the fellow tells us about himself. We want to form an impression of his personality. The more egoistic our interests are, the more cautious we are and the more ready we are to make characterological judgments. But where our social and political interests are concerned, we don't want to take the trouble. We want to be led; we want to sit back; we want someone who tells us what we want to hear, who panders to us, and whom we then reward for doing just that. And so we don't take a close look at him and aren't interested in who he is. But we can learn to look closely. We can learn it in the natural laboratory that all of us, whether we are children, adolescents, or adults, have available to us, the laboratory of our daily experience. We can find just about everything there. All we have to do is want to see it. And then reading can be of some help, too, though it is regrettable that psychology, and especially academic psychology, which has booked so many great successes, has not proved very fruitful in the areas of society and politics. Characterology, the science of character, crucial as it is to politics, to marriage, to friendship, and to education, remains of relatively minor importance in the field of psychology, even though it is far more relevant to life than most of the findings that academic psychology makes. Those findings are some-

times of great theoretical significance, but they are often of pathetically little use to us in facing the immediate, practical problems
of life.

SCHULTZ: I hope you'll excuse me if I bring my own profession
into this conversation (and if I perhaps hugely overestimate its
impact), but shouldn't journalists, if no one else, have a certain
competence in characterology so that at least some of them can
apply and publically articulate the critical perspectives and criteria
we need to free ourselves from illusion when we assess our political
situation and any other processes and developments that affect
us all?

FROMM: Yes, of course. That would be desirable. But there's one
thing we mustn't forget: Making use of characterology requires
courage. It's easy enough to say that this political leadership and
its ideas are good and will help us all. But to say that this man
is a crook, that his policies will lead down the road to destruction,
that his goals are the opposite of what he claims they are, that
his vision is a form of philosophy or religion that runs counter
to everything we think good—to say those things takes courage,
for they are all statements that are often not so easy to prove,
because character can be such a complex thing. Then, too, we tend
to think that negative statements are "unscientific" value judgments
that cannot be proved. We are always ready to make value judgments about matters of taste, but as soon as personalities are involved, people are afraid of saying anything that sounds like a
value judgment. The criticism that their judgments are totally unscientific shakes their confidence in themselves, as if statements
of fact that are at the same time value judgments were somehow
immune from rational examination and discussion.

SCHULTZ: One last question that will repeat and draw together much
of what we have been discussing here. Resistance is one name
for a heightened kind of activity, one we have to be trained for.
But when it comes to social and political issues, what we often
encounter, for a number of reasons, is passivity, lack of interest,
fatalism, a sense of powerlessness, and "refusals," both large and
small, refusals to accept risks and responsibilities, to make decisions, possibly to incur "guilt." This is, unfortunately, not the time
or place to examine those reasons in detail. But I would be grateful

if you could comment briefly on the question of when and where resistance has to begin so that it can become effective long *before* the necessity of assassination has been reached.

FROMM: If you begin your resistance to a Hitler only after he has won his victory, then you've lost before you've even begun. For to offer resistance, you've got to have an inner core, a conviction. You have to have faith in yourself, to be able to think critically, to be an independent human being, a human being and not a sheep. To achieve that, to learn "the art of living and of dying," takes a lot of effort, practice, patience. Like any other skill, it has to be learned. Anyone whose growth takes this direction will also develop the ability to know what is good—or bad—for himself and others, good or bad for him *as a human being,* not good or bad for his success, his acquisition of power or of goods.

The structure of our brains allows us to do something quite unique: We are able to define our optimal goals and put our emotions in the service of those goals. Anyone who takes this path will learn to resist not only the great tyrannies, like Hitler's, but also the "small tyrannies," the creeping tyrannies of bureaucratization and alienation in everyday life. This kind of resistance is more difficult than ever today, for our overall social structure spawns these small tyrannies. In this structure the human being is reduced more and more to a cipher, a cog, a bit player in a bureaucratic scenario. He has no decisions to make, no responsibilities to meet. By and large he does what the bureaucratic machinery has laid out for him. He does less and less thinking, feeling, shaping of his own life. The only things he does think about are products of his own egotism, and they have to do with questions like: How can I get ahead? How can I earn more money? How can I be healthier? He does not ask: What is good for me as a human being? What is good for us as a *polis?* For the Greeks and in the classical tradition those were the great questions that all thought was directed at solving, thought not as an instrument for increasing control over nature but thought as an instrument for answering the question: What is the best way to live? What promotes human growth, the unfolding of our best powers?

Widespread passivity, a lack of participation in the decisions affecting our own lives and our society's life—that is the soil in which fascism or similar movements, for which we usually find names only after the fact, can grow.

133

The Relevance of the Prophets
for Us Today

If we want to discuss the relevance of the prophets for us today we have to begin by asking a few questions. Are the prophets still meaningful for anyone except practicing Christians and Jews? Or to put the question differently: *Shouldn't* they be meaningful to everyone today? Or to go even a little further: Shouldn't they become relevant for us again precisely because they are regarded as irrelevant? Because we live in a time that has no prophets but needs them? But we won't be able to deal with these questions until we have reached some agreement on what a prophet in the Old Testament sense is. Is he a soothsayer who reveals a future that has already been predetermined? Is he a bearer of bad news, not of good or glad tidings? A son of Cassandra? Or is he an oracle, who, like the Delphic oracle, tells us how we should behave, ambiguous though his instructions may be?

First of all, the prophets are not determinists. They do not negate man's will to shape his life and his history. They are seers but not foreseers. Or we could say they are soothsayers, though not in the sense in which we usually use that word but rather in the sense that they say the truth, for that is quite literally what

134

a "soothsayer" does. The truth they speak is that man can choose and has to choose between alternatives and that those alternatives are predetermined. In other words, what a person will do is not predetermined, but the alternatives between which he must choose are predetermined. In biblical times, at the time the prophets spoke, the choices were either to worship the power of the state, of the soil, of everything the idols stood for, or to destroy the state and scatter its citizens.

The people had to choose between those two alternatives, and the prophets articulated those alternatives. But I'd like to stress that what the prophets had to say about those alternatives was not limited, as we today like to think it was, to purely moral or religious issues. They also spoke in terms of *realpolitik* in the strictest sense of that word. They realized that a small Oriental state in the Near East that had lost its spiritual substance, its message, and had become like any other state was doomed to fall in the long run, just as all the other small states before it had been. So there was a choice. The people could choose either to see their state fall or to cease idolizing their state. They could choose between those two possibilities, but the prophets wanted to strip them of their long-harbored illusion that they could have it both ways, that is, that they could have both their ministate and their continuing existence as a people.

We can find a good example of what I mean here in what the judge and prophet Samuel did when the Hebrews said they wanted a king, when they said they wanted to be like all the other nations. Samuel spelled out the alternatives for them. They could choose between oppression for every single person at the hands of an Oriental despot, or they could choose freedom. But the choice between those two alternatives was left to the people, and the people wanted to be like all the other nations. The people wanted a king. And God said to Samuel: Heed what they say, but warn them clearly and show them what a king who would rule them would be like.

That brings us to the third function of the prophets: They protest. Not only do they show what the alternatives are, they also actively warn against the choice that would lead to destruction. They protest against that choice. But once they have stated their message and made their protest, they let people act as they will. Even God does not interfere or perform miracles. The responsibility

135

is left with man, who must shape his destiny himself. The prophet lends aid only in the sense that he tries to articulate the alternatives and call attention to the choices that will lead to disaster.

We are in a similar situation today. We, too, are faced with the choice between a humane society and barbarity, between total nuclear disarmament and total or, at best, massive destruction. Today, too, it would be the prophet's task to spell out the alternatives and to protest against the one that would mean annihilation.

What was the faith of the prophets? The prophets propagated one faith, a belief in one God whose nature comprises truth and justice. But the prophets did not concern themselves primarily with *questions of faith* but rather with *questions of conduct,* the question of how God's principles could be realized in this world. One point of faith, however, was of central importance for the prophets, namely, that God was the one true God. But what does that mean, that God is the one true God? Is that a mathematical problem, one against many? It means that there is a unity, a One, that stands behind all the diversity of things and all the diversity of our own senses and impulses: a One that is the highest principle. But we will grasp the significance of this One in the prophets' thinking only if we take another crucial factor into account, and that factor is the distinction between God and the idols or false gods. Idols are created by men. A god can become an idol, too, if he is worshiped as an idol, as a work of man. God is alive, and the phrase "the living God" recurs over and over again. Idols are things, which is to say, they are dead. As a prophet once said of them: Eyes have they, but they see not; they have ears, but they hear not.

The prophets know that worshiping idols means the enslavement of man. They point out ironically that the idolator starts out with a piece of wood. With half of the piece of wood he makes a fire and bakes a cake. From the other half he makes an idol, and then he worships that piece of wood, that work of his own hands, as if that piece of wood he has shaped were superior to him. And how is it superior to him? Because he has invested all his own powers in the piece of wood, conveyed his powers to it, making himself poor and the idol rich and powerful. And the more powerful that idol is, the poorer the idolater becomes. And to save himself from total impoverishment he has to submit to the idol and win back a share of his inner riches by making himself the idol's slave. In modern philosophical language we call this phenomenon "alienation." The word alienation as Marx and Hegel used it means precisely the same thing as the idea of idolatry did for the prophets: a subjugation of self to things, a loss of the inner self, of freedom, and a self-preoccupation produced by that subjugation. We think that just because we have no Baal or no Astarte we have no idols and are not idolaters. But we forget too easily that our idols simply have other names. They are not called Baal or Astarte but possessions, power, material production, consumer goods, honor, fame, and whatever else it is that people worship these days and enslave themselves to.

Perhaps the contribution of the prophets most important to world history is their vision of a *messianic* period. That was a new and unique vision that would prove to be of immense historical fruitfulness, a vision of "salvation," the salvation of man by means of his own self-realization. The messianic period, as the prophets saw it, meant the time when the curse spoken over man in Eden would be lifted. Part of that curse was man's loss of peace within himself, the ascendancy of his drives, his need to own more and more. The curse also affected the relationship between the sexes. We take it for granted today that men are the ruling sex, but we should keep in mind that in the Bible story the rule of man over woman was imposed as a curse and a punishment. In other words, man did not rule over woman before the curse. And there is much historical evidence to suggest that in prehistoric times there was in fact no domination of man over woman.

The final aspect of the curse I want to mention here is enmity between man and nature, the idea that man has to earn his bread in the sweat of his brow, that work is not a joy but a punishment. This idea has remained a reality for most people up to our own day. And the same curse that condemns man to be at odds with nature is also reflected in the idea that woman will bear her children in pain. Man's sweat and the pain of childbirth for woman are the two symbols that represent the humbling and punishment of humankind in the biblical curse. As I mentioned before, we regard those conditions as natural and inevitable today, but the authors of the Bible did not see them that way at all.

What was this messianic idea the prophets had? It was to establish a new peace that was more than just the absence of war; it was to establish a state of solidarity and harmony among individuals, among nations, between the sexes, between man and nature, a state in which, as the prophets say, man is not taught to be afraid. We forget all too easily that aggression is a consequence of our fear. We are taught to be afraid at every step we take, to mistrust others, to expect the worst. The prophets were radical enough to say that aggression will disappear only when fear disappears. And that fits in with their vision of the messianic age. In their eyes, that would be a time of abundance—not of luxury, but of abundance in the sense that for the first time the table would be set for everyone who wanted to eat at it, for everyone who, as a human being, had the right to sit at that table and join in the shared meal with all other human beings. Another characteristic of the messianic age as the prophets saw it would be not only that people would live in peace and harmony, that they would be free of greed and jealousy and no longer in conflict with themselves and nature, but also that life would have a new goal, a new purpose. And that goal would not be the acquisition of what we need to live in the physical sense. The meeting of those needs is a problem that will always be with us but one that is open to solution. What the prophets were concerned with was knowing God fully. Or to put this idea in nontheological terms: Their goal was for man to develop his psychic powers, his reason, and his life to their full extent; for him to be free and centered in himself; for him to become everything a human being is capable of becoming.

That messianic age is in a certain sense a re-creation of the paradisiacal state. But the paradisiacal state stood at the beginning of history or—if you will—of prehistory. That paradisiacal harmony held sway before man had experienced himself as an individual apart from other individuals. It was a harmony of human underdevelopment, of primitiveness, of a primal, prehistorical unity. The messianic age is a return to that harmony, but only when and after man has fully realized himself in history. The messianic age will not mark the end of history, but it will in a way represent the first beginnings of truly human history, for in it all those things that have kept man from being fully human will have been overcome.

I spoke earlier of the great seminal influence the messianic idea has had on the development of humankind. Perhaps there is no other idea that has had a greater influence on our development. I do not want to go into detailed questions here or raise controversial ones, but I do think I can fairly say that Christianity and socialism have both been profoundly influenced by the messianic idea, though they have each given different expression to it and have in some ways deviated from what I have just outlined as the essence of it.

The messianic idea has been kept alive throughout history. It has been struck down time and again; it has been corrupted time and again, as it has been in Christianity, for example. But it has never died out; it has always remained alive as a seed. We can see that in many ways today. Socialism provides us with another example. The humanistic socialism of Marx has been rapidly and totally corrupted in the so-called socialistic countries. But even in that case the seed has not dried up completely; even there we can see how the secular version of the messianic idea that we find in Marxist socialism but not in Social Democratic or communistic socialism, how this seed comes back to life over and over again, even if only in individual people. It is probably no exaggeration to say that modern history would hardly be conceivable without the immense influence the messianic idea has exerted on it; and modern history cannot be fully understood either, unless we look closely at where and how this idea has triumphed and where and how it has been corrupted.

For this reason we can say that the prophets are of the greatest relevance to us today. They are relevant not only for this reason but also because, as I stressed earlier, the choices we face today are essentially quite similar to the ones people faced at the time of the prophets. We, too, have to see what the alternatives are; we, too, have to choose. And if we want to have some sense of what the relevance of the prophets for us is, then we cannot occupy ourselves exclusively with current events; we have to really *read* the prophets. They make extremely relevant and, if I may say so, extremely exciting reading, and they have much more to tell us about the contemporary world than do many news reports that claim to be up to the minute and to show us the present as it is—but do not *illuminate* the present.

Who Is Man?

T he question "Who is man"? leads us right to the heart of the
problem. If man were a thing, then we could ask *what* he is and
define him the way we define an object in nature or an industrial
product. But man is not a thing and cannot be defined the way
we define a thing. But despite this, man is often seen as a thing.
He is described as a worker, a factory manager, a doctor, and so
on. But such descriptions tell us only what an individual's social
function is. In other words, man is defined in terms of his place
in society.

Man is not a thing; he is a living being caught up in a continual
process of development. At every point in his life he is not yet
what he can be and what he may yet become.

Although man cannot be defined the way we define a table
or a clock, he does not evade definition entirely. We can say more
about him than that he is not a thing but is a living process. The
most important aspect of a definition of man is that his thinking
can reach beyond the satisfaction of his physical needs. For him
thought is not—as it is for an animal—simply a means for procuring
desired goods; it is also a means for exploring the reality of his
own being and of the world around him, independent of his likes

or dislikes. In other words, man not only has intelligence, which animals have, too, but also possesses reason, which he can use to perceive the truth. When man lets himself be guided by his reason, he acts in his own best interests both as an intellectual and as a physical being.

But we know from experience that many people, blinded by greed and vanity, do not act rationally in their private lives. Worse yet, the actions of nations are guided even less by reason, because demagogues are only too ready to let the citizen forget that he will bring his city and his world to ruin if he gives credence to demagogues. Many nations have gone to their destruction because they were not able to free themselves from the irrational emotions that were determining their behavior and because they were not able to learn the way of reason. The crucial task that the prophets of the Old Testament performed was not, as many people think it was, to predict the future. It was to proclaim the truth and thus indirectly suggest what the future consequences of the people's present actions would be.

Since man is not a thing that we can describe from the outside, as it were, we have to turn to our own personal experience as human beings to define him. The question "Who is man?" therefore obliges us to ask, "Who am I?" If we want to avoid the mistake of treating man as a thing, the only answer we can give to the question of "Who am I?" is "a human being."

Most people have never taken cognizance of their identity as human beings. They create all sorts of illusory images of themselves, their qualities, and their identity. They will often respond to our question with "I'm a teacher," "I'm a worker," "I'm a doctor." But that information about a person's work tells us nothing about *that person himself* and contains no clues that will help us answer the question "Who is he?" "Who am I?"

Here we come upon still another difficulty. We all have a certain social, moral, and psychological orientation. When and how can I know whether a direction someone has taken will be his permanent direction or whether some powerful experience will be able to change his orientation? Do people reach a point at which they are so firmly set in their ways that it is correct to say of them that they are who they are and will never change? Statistically it may be possible to say that of a lot of people. But can we say it about everyone right up to the day of his death, and can we say it if we consider that he might have changed if he had lived longer?

We can define man in still another way. He is guided by two kinds of emotions and drives. One kind is biological in origin and is basically the same in all people. It includes everything that comes under the heading of requirements for survival: the need to satisfy hunger and thirst, the need for protection, the need for some form of social structure, and, to a far lesser degree, the need for sexual fulfillment. The emotions of the second type are not rooted in biology and are not the same for everyone. Those emotions—emotions like love, joy, solidarity, envy, hatred, jealousy, competitiveness, greed, and so on—take rise from different social structures. With hate, we have to distinguish between reactive and endogenous hate. I understand those terms as parallels to reactive and endogenous depression. Reactive hate is a response to an attack on or a threat to oneself or one's group, and it usually passes once the danger is past. Endogenous hate is a character trait. A person filled with this kind of hate is always searching for new ways to act out this hate.

Unlike the biologically based emotions, the socially generated emotions I have just been discussing are products of specific social structures. In a society where an exploitive minority dominates a defenseless, impoverished majority, there is hatred on both sides. It is obvious enough that the exploited majority will feel hatred. The hatred of the dominant minority, however, is fueled by fear of the vengeance the oppressed may someday take. Furthermore, the minority has to hate the masses in order to stifle their own feelings of guilt and justify their exploitation. Hate will not disappear as long as justice and equality are lacking. Similarly, truth cannot prevail as long as people have to lie to justify their violations of the principles of equality and justice.

Some people claim that principles like equality and justice are ideologies that have developed in the course of history and are not part of man's basic, natural equipment. I cannot go into a detailed refutation of this argument, but I do want to stress one point that speaks against it: The way people react if a hostile group violates the principles of justice and equality demonstrates that people do have, in their innermost core, a strong sense of those values. The sensitivity of the human conscience is nowhere more evident than in the way most people react to even the most minor violations of justice and equality, provided, of course, that it is not they themselves who are being accused of such violations. And so it is that the conscience finds vehement expression in the accusations that national groups make against their enemies. If people had no natural moral sensibility, how would it be possible to incite them to such violent passions by reporting to them atrocities their enemies have allegedly committed?

Still another definition of man says he is a being in which instinctive governance of behavior has been reduced to a minimum. Man has obviously retained elements of instinctual motivation, as in his need to satisfy hunger and to reproduce. But it is only when the survival of the individual or the community is at stake that man is primarily motivated by instinct. Most of the drives that motivate people—ambition, envy, jealousy, vengeance—take rise in and are fueled by specific social constellations. The fact that those drives can assume priority over even the instinct to survive demonstrates just how powerful they can be. People are often prepared to lay down their lives in the service both of their hatreds and ambitions and of their loves and loyalties.

The most abominable of all human impulses, the need to use another person for one's own ends by virtue of one's power over that person, is little more than a refined form of cannibalism. That urge to use others for our own purposes was unknown in Neolithic societies. For almost everyone alive today, it is practically impossible to imagine that there was ever a historical period when men did not want to exploit and were not exploited. But there was such a time. In the early agricultural and hunter-gatherer cultures everyone had enough to live, and it would have been pointless to accumulate goods. Private property could not yet be invested as capital and used as a source of power. That phase in human thought is reflected in symbolic form in the Old Testament. The children of Israel were fed on manna in the desert. There was enough of it, and everyone could eat as much as he wanted, but manna could not be hoarded. Whatever of it was not eaten the same day spoiled and disappeared. There was no point in speculating on whether more manna would be forthcoming or not. But goods like grain or tools do not disappear. They can be hoarded and do give power to those who have the largest quantities of them. Only when surpluses began to exceed a certain level did it become advantageous for the ruling class to exert power over others and force them to perform work for their rulers and to accept as their own share the bare minimum necessary for existence. The triumph of the patriarchial state made slaves, workers, and women the main victims of exploitation.

Only when man ceases to be a consumer item for his stronger "fellow" man can our cannibalistic, prehistoric period end and our truly human history begin. To effect such a change, we will have to become fully aware of how criminal our cannibalistic ways and customs are. But even full awareness will remain ineffectual if it is not accompanied by equally comprehensive remorse.

Remorse is more than just feeling sorry about something. Remorse is a powerful emotion. A remorseful person feels real disgust for himself and what he has done. True remorse and the shame that accompanies it are the only human emotions that can prevent old crimes from being repeated over and over again. Where there is no remorse, the illusion that no crimes have ever been committed can arise. But where do we find any genuine remorse? Did the Israelites feel remorse for the genocide they perpetrated against the tribes of Canaan? Do the Americans feel remorse for almost completely wiping out the Indians? For millennia man has lived in a system that relieves the victor of remorse because it equates might with right. Every one of us should own up fully to the crimes that our forebears, our contemporaries, or we ourselves have committed, either directly or through our failure to protest them. We should confess those crimes openly, publicly, in ritual form, as it were. The Roman Catholic Church offers the individual an opportunity to confess his sins and thus lets the voice of conscience be heard. But individual confession is not enough, because it does not address the crimes that are committed by a group, a class, a nation, or, most important, a sovereign state, which is not subject to the dictates of individual conscience. As long as we are unwilling to make "confessions of national guilt" we shall continue in our old ways, keeping a sharp eye out for the crimes of our enemies but remaining blind to the crimes of our own people. How can individuals begin to follow the dictates of conscience in any serious way when nations, which profess to be the guardians of morality, act without any regard for conscience at all? What inevitably follows is that the voice of conscience is silenced in every individual citizen, for conscience is no less divisible than truth.

If human reason is to become an effective guide for our actions it cannot be dominated by irrational emotions. Intelligence remains intelligence, even if it is turned to evil purposes. Reason, however, our awareness of reality as it is and not as we would like to see it so that we can exploit it for our own ends—reason in this sense can be effective only to the extent that we can put aside our irrational emotions, that is, to the extent that we as human beings become truly human and that irrational drives cease to be the main motivating force behind our actions.

This brings us to the question of which drives are necessary for the survival of the human race. Aggression and destructiveness may help one group eradicate another and so survive itself, but those drives take on a different meaning if we consider them in the context of humanity as a whole. If aggression spread throughout the entire human population, it would lead not only to the destruction of one group or another but eventually to the eradication of the entire human race. In the past such a thought had no bearing on reality and remained mere idle speculation. Today, our love of life has sunk to a low ebb. The destruction of humankind as a whole is a real possibility, because we now have the means for self-destruction and because we actually toy with the idea of using them. Today we have to realize that the principle of survival of the fittest—the unrestrained will to power of sovereign states— can result in the destruction of all mankind.

In the nineteenth century Emerson said, "Things are in the saddle and ride mankind." Today we can say, "Man has made things his idols, and worship of those idols can destroy him."

We are told repeatedly that there are no limits to the malleability of human beings, and at first glance that would seem to be true. A survey of human behavior through the ages shows us that there is practically no act, from the most noble to the most debased, of which man is not capable and has not actually performed. But the thesis on the malleability of human beings has to be qualified. Any behavior that does not serve a person's growth, his progress toward complete self-realization, takes its toll. The exploiter fears the exploited. The murderer fears the isolation his deed condemns him to, even if that isolation does not take the form of isolation in prison. The destroyer fears his conscience. The joyless consumer fears living without being truly alive.

Implicit in the claim that man is endlessly malleable is the possibility that he can be physiologically alive but crippled in a human sense. Such a person will be unhappy. He will experience no joy. He will be filled with bitterness, and bitterness will make him destructive. Only if he can be freed from this vicious circle will he again be open to the possibility of joy. If we put aside congenital pathological conditions, we can say that human beings are psychically healthy at birth. They become crippled only at the hands of others who want to exert total control over them, who hate life, and who cannot bear to hear joyous laughter. If a child then becomes a cripple, they feel justified in their hostile attitude toward the child, and they regard their hostility as a consequence of the child's ill behavior, not as its cause.

Why would anyone want to make someone else a cripple? The answer to that question lies in what I have said about the cannibalism that is still present in our society today. A psychically crippled person can be exploited more easily than a strong one. The strong person can strike back; the weak one cannot. He is at the mercy of malevolent people in power. The more a ruling group can make psychic cripples of those they dominate, the easier it is for them to exploit their underlings, using them to promote their own purposes.

Because man is gifted with reason, he can analyze his experience critically and see what promotes his development and what hinders it. He works for as harmonious a growth of all his mental and physical powers as he can possibly attain, with the ultimate goal of achieving wellbeing. The opposite of wellbeing is depression, as Spinoza demonstrated. This would suggest that joy is a product of reason, and depression is what results from an incorrect way of life. That finds the clearest of confirmation in the Old Testament, where it is interpreted as grave sin on the part of the Israelites that their lives are joyless even though they live in the midst of abundance.

The basic assumptions of industrial society are in conflict with human wellbeing. What are those assumptions?

The first basic assumption is that nature has to be controlled. But didn't preindustrial society control nature, too? Clearly it did; otherwise, man would have starved to death long ago. But the way we control nature in industrial society is different from the way agricultural societies controlled it. That has been particularly true since industrial society has used technology to control nature. Technology makes use of the human capacity for thought to produce things. It is the male substitute for the female womb. That is why the beginning of the Old Testament describes how God created the world through his word. In the older Babylonian myth of the creation it is the Great Mother who gives birth to the world.

The second basic assumption of industrial society is that human beings can be exploited by means of force, rewards, or—most often—a combination of both.

146

The third assumption is that economic activity has to be profitable. In industrial society the profit motive is not primarily an expression of personal greed but rather a test for the correctness of economic behavior. We do not produce goods to be used, although most goods have to have some utilitarian value if they are to be salable. We produce goods in order to make a profit. The end result of my economic activity has to be that I earn more than I have to spend for the production or the acquisition of marketable goods. It is a common error to represent the profit motive as a personal psychological trait peculiar to greedy people. Desire for profit can, of course, be just that, but such a view of the profit motive does not typify the norm in a modern industrial society. Profit is simply a proof of correct economic behavior and hence a criterion for competence in business.

A fourth trait, which is a classic characteristic of industrial societies, is competition. History has shown, however, that as a result of the increasing centralization and size of some concerns—and as a result of illegal but nonetheless existing price setting—competition between large concerns has given way to cooperation. Where competition does exist it is more likely to occur between two small retail stores than between two industrial concerns. In our entire modern economic order there are no emotional ties left between seller and buyer. In earlier times there was a special relationship between a merchant and his customer. The merchant was interested in his customer, and the sale was more than a financial transaction. The businessman felt a certain satisfaction in selling his customers an item that was useful and appealing. That still happens today, of course, but it is the exception and limited primarily to small, old-fashioned shops. In an expensive department store the salespeople smile politely. In a cheap one, they stare indifferently into space. I hardly need point out that the smile in the expensive store is false and is part of the overhead reflected in the higher prices.

The fifth point I want to mention is that the capacity for sympathy has shrunk in our century. And I should perhaps add that the capacity to suffer has shrunk with it. I don't mean by that, of course, that people suffer less today than they used to. But they are so alienated from themselves that they are no longer fully conscious of their suffering. Like someone with chronic physical pain, they come to accept their suffering as given and perceive it only when it increases beyond its normal intensity. But we should not forget that suffering is the only emotion that appears to be truly common to all human beings, indeed, perhaps to all sentient beings. For that reason, a suffering person who recognizes how widespread suffering is can feel the consolation of human solidarity.

There are many, many people who have never known happiness. But there are none who have never suffered, no matter how doggedly they have struggled to repress their own awareness of their suffering. Sympathy is inseparable from love for humanity. Where there is no love there can be no sympathy. Indifference is the opposite of sympathy, and we can describe indifference as a pathological state with schizoid tendencies. What passes as love for another individual often proves to be nothing but a dependency on that person. Anyone who loves only one person really loves none.

Index

In this, his last work, Erich Fromm sums up a lifetime of rich experience as a social critic, a psychoanalyst, and one of our most inspired commentators on the foibles and frailties of the human condition.

For the Love of Life is based on a series of reflective radio talks Fromm delivered a few short years before his death; speaking with a refreshing spontaneity, he confronts issues ranging from the affluence and ennui of modern society to the meaning of Hitler's personality and the relevance of the prophets today. Here as well are sharp insights into the problem of human growth in a world of "manufactured needs"; the origins of aggression; the crisis in patriarchal society; the universal language of dreams; and the uses of psychology in everyday life.

Seasoned with ideas and insights from Freud, Marx, Camus, Emerson, Weber, and many more great thinkers, Fromm's words have a compelling immediacy and vitality that testify to his genius both as a teacher and a storyteller. Throughout, he speaks with an intense awareness of life's pains and tragedies, yet offers a courageous, life-affirming message about the strengths of self, family, and community, and above all about the transcending power of love. Anyone concerned with the art of living will find his thoughts provocative, his advice sage, and his guidance gentle, down to earth, and infused with hope.

analyst, he was also renowned as a teacher, lecturer, biblical scholar, and antinuclear activist. His many books include the bestselling *The Art of Loving* as well as *Escape from Freedom, Man for Himself, Psychoanalysis and Religion, To Have or to Be?*, and *Anatomy of Human Destructiveness*. Erich Fromm died in Muralto, Switzerland in 1980.